D1389866

THE 🛡 TIMES

QUOTES
of the
WEEK

THE TIMES QUOTES *of the* WEEK

Introduced by Philip Howard

Cartoons by Jonathan Pugh

TIMES BOOKS

HarperCollins*Publishers*
77–85 Fulham Palace Road
Hammersmith
London W6 9JB

The HarperCollins website address is
www.**fire**and**water**.com

First published 2002

Reprint 10 9 8 7 6 5 4 3 2 1 0

ISBN 0 00 712750 2

British Library Cataloguing in Publication Data
A catalogue record for this book is available from
the British Library

Text design by Clare Crawford

Printed and bound in Great Britain by
Omnia Books Ltd, Glasgow G64

Introduction
by
Philip Howard

Some measure history by anniversaries. Others by kings and queens, or parliaments or presidents. For others, photograph albums and family trees preserve flotsam of the past from the torrent of time. Most of us, like J. Alfred Prufrock, measure out our lives with coffee spoons – or these days cappuccinos in cardboard carry-outs. Language is the defining human attribute. So quotations are the most evocative pointers on the clockface of history. You have only to quote: "Here's looking at you, kid," or: "Man your ships, and may the force be with you," or: "We are not amused," or: "We owe a cock to Aesculapius", in order to put us in the picture of times past.

Quotations record our lives and times as we race through the present blindfold into the future. So the quotations of the week in the *Who Said What* column in *The Times* are the abstracts and brief chronicles of our time. They are the first things that I turn to on a Saturday morning. They are the first literary draft of history in the words of celebrities and "ordinary people". (NB: Nobody is ordinary.) Quotations record the historic events and the trivia. They are momentous and terrible, funny or odd. All that they have in common is that in the daily tsunami of words, they caught the attention of journalists, who are trained as fishers of news.

Of course, he who fills his head with other people's words will find no place where he may put his own. Who said that? A Moorish proverb, I am told. But quotation is our national vice (Evelyn Waugh). Quotation is the parole of literary men all over the world? Easy-peasy, and Sam specified "classical" quotation. "Don't quote

Latin; say what you have to say, and then sit down"? The advice of
the Duke of Wellington to a new MP.

The four years covered by this book of quotations (1998–2001)
are rich in disasters, terrible in terrorism, disturbed even in
peacetime. That sentence was an adaptation of Tacitus on the Year of
the Four Emperors, 69 AD and onwards. So enormity (correct usage,
not enormousness, but enormous wickedness, chaps) darkens the
end of the book after September 11. But our quotations cover local,
national and other international affairs as well. They include the
sayings of the great and the good, but also of the celebs, the
nonentities and the bad, and the man on the Clapham omnibus and
the woman on the donkey in Kabul. Hear the wisdom and the
waffle of Popes and Presidents, celebs and nonents. Some of their
quotes are eloquent and lapidary, others are funny and ephemeral.
Jonathan Pugh, our pocket Hogarth, illustrates why a good picture
is worth a thousand quotes. All these quotations catch the attention
and linger in the memory. Historians a thousand years hence will
find them a unique window on the way we live now. For us who
have lived through them, This is Your Life. Enjoy. Wonder. Admire.

PHILIP HOWARD

1998

As the President of the United States walks with Hillary and the Blairs into the State Dining Room, his height, his sleekness, his newly cropped, iron-filing hair, and the intensity of his blue eyes project a kind of avid inclusiveness that encircles every jaded celebrity he passes
— *Tina Brown, editor of the* New Yorker.

History shows that attempts to establish world hegemony are always shortlived
— *Boris Yeltsin on the build-up of American and British forces in the Gulf.*

Disqualifying a snowboarder for having traces of marijuana is like disqualifying a darts player for having traces of lager
— *British snowboard retailer Mon Barbour on Canadian gold medallist Ross Rebagliati's positive dope test.*

John feels that this was a cowardly act . . . but he and Pauline [Mrs Prescott] were determined to stay on to see the final performance by Fleetwood Mac
— *David Prescott on his father's reaction to being drenched at the Brit Awards.*

Poor Enoch, driven mad by the remorselessness of his own logic
— *The late Ian McLeod MP, quoted in* The Times *obituary of Enoch Powell.*

I think it's knitting together. I can sneeze now without feeling I'm splitting apart
— *The Prince of Wales on his cracked rib.*

You have to have the Ray-Bans, and a good four-wheel drive — Red Cross Land Cruisers are the ones to be seen in
— *Aid worker Denise Meredith talking to* Vogue *about "aid chic".*

Luvvies have been whining for more Government cash since the Roman emperors hired them
— *Denis MacShane, Foreign Office PPS, quoted by William Rees-Mogg in* The Times.

This is to Gateshead what the Eiffel Tower is to Paris
— *Gateshead councillor Pat Connaty on Anthony Gormley's massive* Angel of the North *statue.*

Unfortunately we are unable to continue with the scheduled service because we cannot get the shed doors open
— *Platform announcement by Chiltern Railways.*

Parents who send their children to private schools should be whipped
— *David Blunkett, Secretary of State for Education and Employment.*

We now understand that some people perceive that it contains references to drugs
— *Sony when withdrawing a snowboarding computer game advert with words: "Powder, my body yells, aches for powder. I need the rush, the buzz. I have to get higher than the last time."*

Extraordinarily puerile
— *Prime Minister's spokesman on John Redwood's criticism of the City of London for honouring Chancellor Helmut Kohl.*

It should have said Hague
— *The Guardian clarifying a headline: "Haig to drop old guard in shadow reshuffle".*

It's chips the lads want. I ask the Kuwaitis for them every day but I just can't get them ▼

— *RAF Regiment catering officer at Ali al-Salem airbase, 40 miles from Kuwait-Iraq border.*

Everything we own is now at the bottom of the ocean
— *Shipwrecked sailors Doreen and Peter Cheek.*

Week ending February 28, 1998

You bastards, what are you doing? You'll be getting Shula pregnant next
— *Archers' fan reacting to the death of John Archer.*

They make such an issue of being a young government and yet they are taking away a fundamental right of being young
— *Blur lead singer Damon Albarn protesting at Labour's plans for higher education.*

We are not a Winter Games nation
— *Simon Clegg, chief executive of the*
British Olympic Association — Britain
came last in the medal-winners table.

They should give Sean a peerage
— *Sir John Mills on the controversy about*
not giving Sean Connery a knighthood.

We have a deal
— *Kofi Annan's spokesman after the UN*
Secretary General persuaded Saddam
Hussein to allow UN weapons inspectors
access to suspected chemical weapons sites.

If cricket wants to face the future, it
must let "the ladies" into Lord's
— The Guardian *on MCC decision not*
to admit women.

A fantastic day out
— *Tony Blair on the Millennium Dome.*

If it is a failure we will never be
forgiven
— *Peter Mandelson on the Dome.*

This insane piece of statist
grandiloquence
— *Playwright David Hare on ditto.*

An oversight
— *Conservative Central Office on*
William Hague's failure to tax a car
bought for his wife.

An initial outlay of 50p has become
the answer to my prayers
— *Anonymous woman who bought a*
brooch for 50p and sold it for £13,225.

Now that cinemas are smoke-free
and offering some great British films,
I have returned to their seats
— *John Redwood.*

They do not come much bigger than
this
— *Sir Elton John after being knighted by*
the Queen.

Week ending March 7, 1998

Let their friendship stand as a symbol
of the peace process
— *Tony Blair on the shooting by loyalist*
gunmen of best friends Damien Trainor, a
Catholic, and Philip Allen, a Protestant,
at Poyntzpass in Co Armagh.

You're not talking about something
down at the DIY store
— *The Lord Chancellor describing his new*
£300-a-roll wallpaper.

It was only £5,000
— *Official refuting reports that Agriculture*
Minister Jack Cunningham's new desk
cost £10,000.

It seems nothing is sacred where
European regulations are concerned,
not even the body and blood of
Christ
— *From* L'Avvenire, *the Italian Catholic*
daily, on an EU plan to introduce sell-by
dates for Communion wafers.

We hope Mr Howell will accept the
invitation as the party will be outside
— *Buckingham Palace spokesman after a*

guest was injured by falling plaster during an honours presentation.

So the Universe began as a tiny particle. Would Professor Hawking explain . . . how this particle got there?
— *Letter to* The Times.

Got where?
— *Subsequent letter to* The Times.

He was a kind of comedic meteor
— *Fellow actor Frank Kelly on the late Dermot "Father Ted" Morgan.*

Week ending March 14, 1998

Being a good Environment Minister, I put all my papers in the bin
— *Deputy Prime Minister John Prescott referring to thefts of financial documents from his dustbin.*

Ever had the feeling you've been cheated?
— New Musical Express *pits Brit pop stars against Tony Blair.*

He had exactly the right intuition as to how to please a French audience
— *French TV presenter Christine Ockrent on Tony Blair.*

What cricket needs is people to run the game who have a better understanding of humanity
— *John Cryer MP on sex-discrimination scandals at Lord's.*

If you have information which you want to give to the Security Service, please hold the line
— *Recorded greeting on MI5's first published phone line.*

The quickest, cheapest option without any consideration of the consequences for the environment or the future
— *Great Brington parish council reacting to Earl Spencer's proposal to build a huge carpark for visitors to the Diana museum at Althorp.*

Quiet. Too quiet. It must be a trap
— *German official joking about the UK's low-key "Stealth Presidency" of the European Union.*

"A new, scrapie-like syndrome"
— *Words removed at Minister of Agriculture's insistence from the first published research describing BSE in 1987.*

Frankly appalling
— *Parliament's public accounts committee on inefficiency at the Child Support Agency.*

If the evidence stands up, it gives us a new dimension of their capabilities
— *Natural History Museum on reports that Homo erectus was smarter than Homo sapiens had assumed.*

Week ending March 21, 1998

No, no, it's fine, honey, it's fine
— *John Travolta, playing the President, after being slapped seven times by first*

lady *Emma Thompson during filming of Primary Colors.*

I remember thinking "what in the world is he doing?"
– *Kathleen Willey, 51, alleging sexual harassment by President Clinton.*

For supposedly intelligent boys they did not pick the best place to smoke cannabis
– *Thames Valley Police spokesman referring to two Etonians caught smoking outside Windsor police station.*

If it's good enough for beagles, it's good enough for me
– *Richard Littlejohn discussing smoking in* The Sun.

Mr Brown might reflect that 80 per cent of the cost of petrol is tax while only 25 per cent of the cost of champagne is tax
– *RAC spokesman commenting on budget proposals for motoring.*

There were, like, lots of mentions of Prudence – who's she?
– *School pupil, overheard on a train discussing Gordon Brown's budget speech.*

I gave her a kiss but it wasn't much of one because I still had my lion's head on
– *Gavin Lucas who dresses up as Hercules the Lion, Aston Villa's mascot, after being sent off for going too far with Miss Aston Villa just before the match against Atletico Madrid.*

I have just got back from a detox clinic
– *Matthew Roman before being arrested for registering eight times over the blood-alcohol limit in a police breath test.*

Week ending March 28, 1998.

I've got a lot of killing to do
– *Mitchell Johnson, 13, before gunning down four children and one teacher in Arkansas.*

No doubt you will urge the British Legion to drop their Poppy appeal in case everyone starts taking opium
– *Anita Roddick replies to criticism from Tory MP Ann Widdecombe that the Body Shop's new hemp-derived products will attract youth to cannabis.*

He's not been out of trouble since the day he left you
– *Margaret Cook's mother, to her daughter, former wife of the Foreign Secretary.*

I think they're bastards for not coming
– *Rod Stewart on the failure of Hollywood's A-list stars to attend a fundraising ball in memory of Diana, Princess of Wales.*

There was a problem with the ignition system
– *Rocket builder Steve Bennett, whose Starchaser III space probe rose 200ft and then set a large swath of Dartmoor alight.*

That was my first lesson in applied socialism
– *Tony Blair telling the French*

Parliament how, in a Paris bar, he was the only waiter putting his tips in the kitty.

These events are totally out of character as anyone who knows them knows
— Newcastle United boss Sir John Hall on insulting remarks made by his son, Douglas, and Freddy Shepherd.

I'm categorically a big loser tonight
— Minnie Driver on her failure to win a best supporting actress Oscar.

I think he would need a bit more styling before we put him on the cover
— Marina Gask, editor of teen girls' magazine Sugar, *on the attraction of Prince William.*

Week ending April 4, 1998

Is this an April Fool's joke?
— President Clinton on hearing that Paula Jones' sex harassment case had been dismissed.

We get tragedies by the truckload
— Criminal Injuries Compensation Authority boss explaining a minimal award to Josie Russell after the hammer attack which killed her mother and sister.

Nothing ever surprises me
— Prime Minister's press secretary Alastair Campbell reacting to accusations that he was horrid to ministers.

He was driving like a prat
— Jason Humble, allegedly, on the man he was accused of killing by shunting his car into oncoming traffic.

I would be horrified if a tin-pot company treated an employee like this
— Frank Field MP, on Westminster Abbey's suspension of organist Dr Martin Neary.

Her fate is a lesson to us all
— Fraser Kemp MP joins the campaign to free Coronation Street's *Deirdre from jail.*

That was one hell of a result tonight
— Leeds United player after the team's plane crashlanded.

No one can knock the curry restaurant sector . . . and be taken seriously
— Tandoori magazine's fulsome apology for calling Indian waiters "miserable gits".

We are not suckers
— Israeli Prime Minister explains his decision not to revive the Middle East peace process.

This is not a time to give in to short-term pressures
— Chancellor Gordon Brown replying to complaints about the strength of sterling.

Week ending April 11, 1998

Zip me up before you go go
— Sun headline on pop star George Michael's arrest for alleged sex act in a public lavatory.

Thank God for the paparazzi. They can kill but they can also save

– *Rolling Stone Ron Wood after being
rescued from a burning motorboat by
photographers following him.*

He should be sent away – to the Isle
of Wight for instance
– *East End mother on released
paedophile Sidney Cooke.*

This is no time for soundbites . . . I feel
the hand of history on our shoulders
– *Prime Minister Tony Blair on the
Northern Ireland peace talks.*

The best time [to have sex] was
when there were flying operations
because there was lots of noise
– *Evidence at court-martial of
Lieutenant-Colonel Commander Keith
Pople accused of an affair with
Lieutenant-Commander Karen Pearce.*

Grant came back because he loves
me, pure and simple
– *Della Bovey after temporarily winning
her husband back from TV presenter
Anthea Turner.*

I think the Spice Girls are like a
drug. It's like heroin. . . . They can't
help but absorb it, even if they are
sick of it
– *Geri Halliwell suggests young fans are
addicted to her band.*

Frankly I take umbrage at this. It
makes us sound like a Third World
village without any water
– *Resident of Gloucester housing estate
to which Oxfam has sent an Indian aid
worker.*

The newspaper was aware when it
published it that the biography was a
spoof
– The Daily Telegraph *refers to* The
Sunday Telegraph*'s reprinting on April 5
of long extracts from William Boyd's
hoax biography of "artist" Nat Tate.*

Week ending April 18, 1998

It is presumably quite difficult to
burn a bail
– *Lord Darnley, whose mother-in-law's
incinerated veil is now thought to
constitute the Ashes.*

There is no reason why people
cannot come to France and enjoy the
atmosphere of the matches
– *French tourism minister Michelle
Demessine invites ticketless football fans
to France for the World Cup.*

If they don't want our money,
Jamaica and Belize are just itching
for it
– *Passenger on a lesbian cruise ship
banned from visiting the Bahamas.*

It is good for David Blunkett to
experience what teachers have to put
up with from unruly pupils
– *Union leader Nigel de Gruchy on
heated NUT conference in Blackpool.*

If they say "Mummy would have
wanted this", I would like to do
something
– *Earl Spencer on consulting Prince
William and Prince Harry about his
Diana memorial plans at Althorp.*

Bicycles do take up space and time
to tie up and look after
— *P&O justifies its decision to charge for bicycles on cross-Channel ferries.*

What, I should like to know, is so
great about being cool, anyway?
— *Comedian Ben Elton criticises the New Labour rebranding of the UK as Cool Britannia.*

The mother of all treacheries
— *Ian Paisley on the Northern Ireland peace agreement.*

Well done Trimble ▼
— *New graffito in Belfast.*

No technology in the world is proof
against them

— *Timber treatment expert on a colony of termites found in Devon, four years after it had been "destroyed".*

Week ending April 25, 1998

The system for tickets is well-
rehearsed and organised
— *World Cup official on the chaotic telephone hotline for buying tickets.*

The chances of getting through are
about one in two million
— *Academic football fan's analysis of the ticket system.*

The Government thinks beef on the
bone is too unsafe for the Scots but
that Dounreay, which is falling apart,
is a convenient dump for nuclear waste

– *Alex Salmond, Scottish Nationalist Party leader, on secret deal to reprocess former Soviet plutonium.*

I didn't want to do it because your prestige in cinema tends to drop if you do television
– *Sean Connery turns down a part in the American sitcom* Friends.

It is important he gets a good night's sleep
– *German embassy explains why it sent officials to jump up and down on hotel beds in Cardiff where their 6ft 5in Chancellor will stay in June.*

It could be of particular use to school children
– *English Heritage justifies listing a rabbit warren as a historical monument.*

Geoffrey was very persistent in his marriage proposals
– *Italian actress Annabella Incontrera refers to an alleged affair with the multimillionaire Paymaster General.*

It's getting a bit like Chicago
– *P&O describing smuggling and crime at Dover.*

The three-piece-suite mentality still dominates
– The Times *on Lord Irvine's newly decorated official apartments.*

Week ending May 2, 1998

She is truly representative of the city
– *The local council explains why it used a picture of Marge Potter, 67, to promote Birmingham.*

You can actually snore in space
– *Nasa astronaut Dave Williams quashes speculation that gravity is required for snoring.*

We have away games. We play away matches
– *The Duchess of York explains how she and Prince Andrew manage their amours.*

I don't care if you are Alan Shearer or the Pope, you don't do something like that
– *Leicester City manager Martin O'Neill criticises the Newcastle player's conduct.*

I am effectively being evicted
– *Paul Burrell, butler to Diana, Princess of Wales, on being told by Buckingham Palace officials to leave his grace-and-favour home in London.*

I would stake my life on the fact that he is dead
– *Lady Lucan on her missing husband.*

We would still like to speak to Lord Lucan in connection with our inquiries into the death of Sandra Rivett
– *Scotland Yard spokesman.*

I can't wait to see my Dad although I know he will stink
– *Alicia Hempleman-Adams, aged eight, whose father, David, has just skied to the North Pole.*

This money is absolutely inifinitesimal in comparison with the offers she has had from the very same newspapers which have been screaming loudest
– *Gitta Sereny defends her decision to pay Mary Bell for collaborating with her book* Cries Unheard.

Week ending May 9, 1998

Unredeemable trainspotting vacuity overlaid by the gloss of management theory
– *John Redwood's leadership campaign boss Hywel Williams on William Hague.*

A bit like the *Titanic*
– *Edinburgh resident imagines the interior of the former Royal Yacht* Britannia.

They were so generous, so courteous. We simply couldn't eat everything put before us
– *David Mitchell describes how he and his family were kindly treated for 17 days by kidnappers in Yemen.*

No amount of football can make up for the lack of a normal life and female company
– *Vatican insider on tension within the Swiss Guard.*

Women are around all the time but World Cups come only every four years
– *Former Chelsea player Peter Osgood explains his priorities.*

One drunken person recording another bunch of drunks does not constitute business deals
– *George Harrison gives evidence to halt sales of a 1962 recording of the Beatles in Hamburg.*

It was all fantasy. It was like a gangster movie
– *Colombian TV researcher Adriana Quintana on Carlton's award-winnning drug-smuggling documentary.*

The head appears faded in a bit of a mist
– *President of the Royal Society of Portrait Painters on the latest portrait of the Queen.*

As far as I am concerned this is done and dusted
– *Leicester City's Neil Lennon dismisses claims that Alan Shearer kicked him on purpose during a match last week.*

Week ending May 16, 1998

Peter Penfold is a hero to everyone in this country
– *Sierra Leone newspaper hails the British High Commissioner.*

Such a shameful event will not take place in Jerusalem
– *City's deputy mayor does not welcome the Eurovision Song Contest.*

A lot of the hoo-ha is overblown
– *Tony Blair on the arms-to-Sierra Leone controversy.*

It's me sitting in this house with
£50m in the bank, not you
– *Lord Archer replies to journalist who
asked whether he had any regrets in life.*

I could not jeopardise ten years of
honesty, decency and hard work
– *Former cat burglar Peter Scott pleads
guilty to involvement in the theft of a
Picasso painting.*

Paul loved to be spanked and it was a
big feature of our relationship. I had
to tell him he was a very naughty
boy
– *Gloria Stewart describes her adulterous
relationship with moral campaigner and
journalist Paul Johnson.*

I still believe in family values
– *Paul Johnson admits to the 11-year affair.*

Corrections and clairifications
– *Misprint in* The Guardian's
"corrections and clarifications" feature.

I'd no idea my knickers could be seen
– *Liz Hurley on the revealing dress she
wore to a society wedding.*

With women there is a tremendous
desire to expose themselves. With
men the motive is often some kind
of obscure revenge
– *Auberon Waugh on what motivates
people to write novels.*

It doesn't bother me. The boy won't
do it publicly. It's not a problem
– *Glenn Hoddle declares his indifference
to Paul Gascoigne's smoking habit.*

Every week they delay compensation
they save money because one of us
dies
– *Arthur Titherington, spokesman for
British prisoners-of-war formerly held by
the Japanese.*

Language such as hun and boche is
passé. Our readers don't want that
any more and nor do we
– *Piers Morgan, editor of the* Mirror,
*apologises after Press Complaints
Commission warns papers against
xenophobic headlines during World Cup.*

The resin is flexible, soft, organic, like
a part of the body. It is feminine
– *Architect Gaetano Pesce describes his
proposed memorial to Diana, Princess of
Wales, in Paris.*

I hope they get lots of column inches
– *Onlooker as Greenpeace campaigners
climb Nelson's Column to publicise a
protest against logging in Canada.*

Cooks in the kitchen waiting for the
order
– *Senior official describes the readiness of
nuclear armaments scientists in Pakistan
and India.*

Week ending May 23, 1998

I'm losing
– *Frank Sinatra's last words.*

Either he is an unbelievable athlete
or I have a career as a golf instructor
– *Bill Clinton praises Tony Blair's
aptitude for golf.*

It's definitely art
– Leeds University tutor defends students who spent a £1,100 exhibition grant on what they pretended was a holiday in Spain.

Of course it's not art
– Brian Sewell, London Evening Standard *critic.*

They're totally taking the piss
– Representative of Leeds Student Union which contributed £1,126 to the "art" project.

There are some things the parents of the groom-to-be don't want to see and the bride's nipples are two of them
– The Sun reflects on the transparent dress worn by Emma Noble, fiancée of James Major, to the Bafta awards.

No one has asked about my son Mark who is also getting married
– Terry Major-Ball.

We want to do this in a balanced and sensitive way
– Channel 5 on its proposed TV film about sadistic serial murderers Fred and Rose West.

The stuff that happened is not right for a film. You couldn't film it – it wouldn't be watchable
– Mae West, daughter of Fred West.

Exploit an idiot: rent a room to a football fan
– Poster in Montpellier, France.

I feel like a kebab with onions on
– Paul Gascoigne replies to journalist who asked whether he feels old.

This kind of thing cannot be happening here. They must be forgeries
– French official is shocked when British newspaper purchases genuine tickets for World Cup on black market in Marseilles.

The lottery is now a fact of life
– Colin Campbell QC after the Church of Scotland votes to abandon its stance against accepting lottery money.

He made a "phwoar" kind of noise from the car
– Soldier's wife describes alleged sexual harassment by an army chaplain.

Why doesn't it shut up? Take the batteries out!
– Male response to virtual baby designed to simulate the real thing in an effort to curb teenage pregnancies.

He is already rocking now; he will be rolling on Friday
– Ian Paisley scorns Ulster Unionist leader David Trimble for attending Yes campaign concert organised by U2 lead singer Bono.

The other swans seem to have taken against them
– Keeper on a pair of "homosexual" swans at Abbotsbury Swannery, Dorset.

Becoming a member of the IRA was "fun and exciting"

– The Daily Telegraph *serialises memoir by Sean O'Callaghan who was convicted of two murders and several other criminal offences.*

Week ending May 30, 1998

It was a wonderful protest. I think we got the message across
– *War veteran on demonstration during Emperor Akihito's visit to Buckingham Palace.*

It saddens me that the relationship so nurtured between our two countries should have been marred by the Second World War
– *Emperor Akihito.*

She has become a parrot
– *Democratic Unionist Party leader Ian Paisley on the Queen.*

If grass can grow through cement, love can find you at every time in your life
– *Cher reflects on the difficulty of being a fiftysomething actress on Hollywood.*

We knew our customers would be interested
– *British Airways defends showing soft porn in-flight films.*

Ticket displayed upside down
– *Yorkshire parking warden's reason for fining a motorist £15.*

That's a bit rich, them suing us for firing at them

– *Ministry of Defence responds to reports that the United Kingdom is to be sued by Saddam Hussein.*

I am convinced we will make some positive impact on drug-taking over the next ten years
– *Government drugs "czar" Keith Hellawell.*

He really wants to support a British team
– *Royal family insider on Prince Harry going to the World Cup in France.*

It worries me sometimes that things are a bit too easy for them
– *Tony Blair on his children.*

I don't care who it is, mate, rules are rules
– *Pilot tells Tony Blair to turn off his mobile phone on which he is talking to the Queen during take-off.*

Week ending June 6, 1998

Suddenly my waist wobbled. It was the pager saying ring the leader's office
– *Ann Widdecombe on how she was informed of her appointment to the Shadow Cabinet.*

Lots of love, Geri. PS I'll be back
– *Geri Halliwell's sign-off after leaving the Spice Girls.*

Mentally he's always had a few problems. . . . He had tears in his eyes

and he shook my hand but he was too emotional to take it in
– Glenn Hoddle on Paul Gascoigne's reaction to being left out of the England World Cup squad.

I lost my rag big time . . . kicked the door and the table when Hoddle told me I'd been axed
– Paul Gascoigne.

What a week – first Geri, then Gazza, and now me
– Stuart Higgins, resigning as editor of The Sun.

So many people, so many dead, hundreds injured. This is truly a disaster, a terrible accident
– Chancellor Kohl on German intercity train crash.

You simply don't go up to a hippo and take its baby
– Warden at West Midland Safari Park on attempt to rescue a newborn hippo which fell into water beside its mother and later died.

The show has never had celebrities before
– Three Counties Show spokesman on appearance of porcine escapees Butch and Sundance at showbiz rate of £1,500 each.

£45? If I'd known that was all it would cost, I'd have slapped him twice
– Freddie Starr on being fined for hitting his 18-year-old son.

I like this one but I don't like the big lumpy ones
– Margaret Thatcher on Henry Moore sculptures.

Week ending June 13, 1998

We are not going to be lectured on tax affairs by tax exiles. The sight of ageing hippies on a tax scam telling the Chancellor what to do is not on
– Government source after the Rolling Stones cancelled a British tour because of budget tax reforms.

They hate the term "tax exile". It sounds like someone sitting by a pool in Marbella sipping a pina colada
– Bernard Docherty, spokesman for the Rolling Stones.

She was my girlfriend
– Sir Paul McCartney at the memorial service to his wife Linda at St Martin-in-the-Fields.

I don't think Hoddle is known for his dress sense
– Paul Smith, designer of the England squad's controversial suits.

France has done what it had to do, but nothing more
– Michel Platini, co-president of the World Cup organising committee.

After God, comes football in Brazil
– Footballer Pele on Brazil's industry closing down during the World Cup.

The moral responsibility has to
weigh heavily on the consciences of
all historically sensitive Germans
– *German Foreign Ministry note
apologising for a massacre of thousands of
men, women and children in Herero,
Namibia, in 1904.*

We have a committed relationship
but we haven't married. We want to
set this straight because we've started
getting wedding presents
– *Film-maker David Furnish on rumours
that he has "married" Sir Elton John.*

Oh my God, Charles, it's the Captain
– *Reema Mahabeer, 23, when caught
apparently in flagrante delicto with
company director Charles Watkinson, 51,
on Flight SA233 from London to
Johannesburg.*

Week ending June 20, 1998

If these thugs had any reason at all
we could appeal to it
– *Sports minister Tony Banks on some of
the English football supporters in
Marseille.*

I admit I threw things at the police
but it was not stones. I thought it was
turf
– *Football hooligan James Shayler after
being jailed for two months after rioting
in Marseille.*

A compliment to the English martial
spirit
– *Alan Clark MP on football hooligans.*

I did not deliberately mislead this
House. I did not do it inadvertently
either
– *Foreign Office Minister Baroness
Symons on the arms-to-Africa affair.*

The official dark blue Rovers used
by other summit leaders were too
small to accommodate Herr Kohl
– *Member of the German delegation at
the European Union summit in Cardiff
explains why Chancellor Kohl travels by
bus.*

Mr Lawrence, I wanted to say to you
that I am truly sorry that we let you
down
– *Ian Johnston, Metropolitan Police
assistant commissioner, apologises to
Neville Lawrence for the police's failure to
bring his son's killers to justice.*

I am my mother's daughter
– *The Queen tells Nelson Mandela why
she looks so well.*

The sun is shining uselessly over the
North Sea
– *Weather forecaster Ian McCaskill, who
has just given his last BBC TV forecast.*

It is entirely proper that Richard
Branson's knighthood should be
delayed – so many of his trains are
– *Letter to* The Guardian.

The food is so bad I couldn't wait to
get home
– *American actress Gwyneth Paltrow
criticises the British cuisine.*

Week ending June 27, 1998

That wasn't hooliganism, it was terrorism
– *German football federation boss after French police identified 614 German neo-Nazis in Lens.*

There's only one team that is going to win now, and that is England
– *Kevin Keegan just before Romania scores a winning goal.*

If the parents didn't do it, who did?
– *Au pair Louise Woodward, accused of causing the death of a baby in her care.*

The law should not put police into bedrooms nor coerce gay men to be heterosexual
– *Ann Keen MP in favour of lowering age of consent for homosexuals to 16.*

There is a wave of homosexual triumphalism sweeping the country
– *Richard Littlejohn in* The Sun.

Is this the most dangerous man in Britain?
– The Sun *warns that Tony Blair is in favour of the European single currency.*

Jonathan Dimbleby was the worst prepared popinjay of a reporter I have ever encountered
– *Camille Paglia after storming out of an interview.*

This is the Judy Garland of the 100 metres
– *Former armed robber John McVicar, in*

court to defend Linford Christie's action against him.

To pretend somebody said something when they were supposedly dying? It's monstrous, isn't it?
– *Earl Spencer contests Mohammed Al Fayed's account of Diana's last words.*

It is well known that many media figures enjoy it
– *Naturist Foundation, hosting a kit-off edition of* Gardeners' Question Time.

It is on time, on track and on budget ▼
– *Tony Blair on the Millennium Dome, which is still looking for between £50 and £175 million in private sponsorship.*

MILLENNIUM DOME
PLEASE PLACE YOUR DONATIONS HERE

Week ending July 4, 1998

Yet again I have had to listen to people peddle lies and then watch them walk away
– *Neville Lawrence during the inquiry into the murder of his son Stephen.*

We all know this one is not simply about the parade itself
– *Chairman of Northern Ireland Parades commission on the Orangemen's desire to march along Garvaghy Road, from Portadown, to Drumcree, Co Armagh.*

David Beckham's sending off cost us dearly. I am not denying it cost us the game
– *Glenn Hoddle after England lost to Argentina on penalties.*

This is the worst moment of my career. I want every England supporter to know how deeply sorry I am
– *David Beckham apologises.*

This is the greatest result of my career and hopefully it will boost the morale of the nation
– *Tim Henman on getting through to the Wimbledon semi-finals.*

Nothing short of a disaster
– *Sir Richard Eyre on the Royal Opera House.*

What's the point of traipsing out to W12 late at night so Jeremy can try to persuade the public that I am some kind of criminal

– *Minister quoted by Tony Blair's press spokesman Alastair Campbell in a critique of "sofa TV" political interviews.*

His remarks are, to use his own characteristically sophisticated term in lobby briefings, crap – that's C.R.A.P
– *Jeremy Paxman analyses Alastair Campbell's critique.*

There will be no drinks at the bar
– *Ian Paisley sets the tone for the new Northern Ireland Assembly.*

Week ending July 11, 1998

I will be here until we win. I will be here for the rest of my life if necessary
– *Orangeman digs in at Drumcree.*

Born to walk the Garvaghy Road – No surrender
– *Slogan on Irish baby's bib.*

Roger is a man of complete integrity but excessive goodwill
– *A minister on Tony Blair's policy adviser Roger Liddle, implicated in controversy about improper lobbying.*

I can have tea with Geoffrey Robinson, I can get in to Ed Balls
– *Disgraced lobbyist Derek Draper boasts of his influence with the Paymaster General and the Chancellor's economic adviser.*

Even with my sinuses I can smell the stench coming out of these allegations
– *William Hague on the lobbying controversy.*

Turn it down, I can't even hear myself think
— *Oasis frontman Liam Gallagher distressed by loud music in a nearby car.*

There is no connection between naturism and sex
— *James Scarlett, whose holiday videos of naked people were ruled not obscene.*

This is a betrayal of the British toilet
— *Michael Fabricant MP criticises the "harmonised" Euro-loo standard.*

The possibility of armed conflict and the use of automatic weapons and explosives
— *National Criminal Intelligence Service warns police forces what to expect from feuds between rival motorcycle gangs this summer.*

The Queen is entitled to use the gifts that God has given her to mimic anyone she pleases
— *Ian Paisley on hearing that the Queen does a wickedly funny impersonation of him.*

Week ending July 18, 1998

This is what we mean by education, education, education
— *Chancellor Gordon Brown announces an extra £19 billion for education.*

In the past 12 months too few of our new comedies have been successes
— *John Birt as the BBC bids for a sharply increased licence fee.*

She looked considerably more than three the last time I saw her
— *Editor of the new* International Who's Who, *which lists Scottish model Honor Fraser's date of birth as 1994.*

In Britain if you've got a title then you also don't have any brains
— *Edward Windsor, formerly known as Prince.*

Godzilla, the 400ft turkey
— The Independent *reviews the latest US movie sensation.*

I claim this victory for the National Front
— *French far-rightwing leader Jean-Marie Le Pen muscles in on France's football glory.*

The 15-minute walk down the Garvaghy Road would be in the shadow of the coffins of three little boys who wouldn't even know what the Orange Order is about
— *The Order's chaplain for Co Armagh.*

I don't know who Tony Blair is but I do know the cost of fags
— *12-year-old mother interviewed by* The Mirror.

I hope I don't die before Harry Secombe. I don't want him singing at my funeral
— *Spike Milligan jokes at memorial service for Alf Garnett creator Johnny Speight.*

Just a fun thing
— Tiger Woods after driving 439 yards
from the eighth tee at Royal Birkdale
while practising for the Open.

Week ending July 25, 1998

When you do a gas the gas comes
out of the car and if the car's not
moving you get less gas
— John Prescott unveils his transport
white paper in the House of Commons.

I couldn't put into words how much
I hated it. It looked like a cheap set
for some kind of murder mystery
weekend
— Susan Dukes on a surprise decoration
makeover of her dining room by the
BBC's Changing Rooms *series.*

It is inhabited by the young and the
different live there
— Home Office Minister Lord Williams
appeals to peers to think of the "world
outside" when voting on the age of
homosexual consent.

He said he was getting through half a
bottle of vodka before he gets out of
bed in the morning
— Patient at drying-out clinic where
Coronation Street *star Kevin Kennedy*
is being treated.

Silly old fool. I pushed him into a
rose bush for that
— Anna Ford recalls when Sir Robin Day
told her she got a job as newsreader only
because men wanted to sleep with her.

Mum and Dad would have found it
very hard to believe that the house is
now a National Trust property
— Sir Paul McCartney on his childhood
home being opened to the public.

I'm a millionaire right? Well, I
haven't seen a penny of it
— British golfing star Justin Rose on
reports of his newfound status.

The bioelectric shield puts a cocoon
around you. At the edge of the
cocoon is a layer that spins. That
spinning layer is like a gatekeeper.
Any energy that is not compatible
will be diverted
— Dr Charles Brown, inventor of New
Age crystal-filled locket worn by Cherie
Blair, on how his creation works.

Week ending August 1, 1998

In an effort to achieve prompt
resolution of this entire matter the
President will voluntarily provide his
testimony
— President Clinton's lawyer after
agreeing that his client should appear
before a grand jury.

If the last 15 months have taught me
anything it is that the whole Cabinet
— especially the Chancellor — must
share common beliefs on the biggest
of all reforms
— Frank Field MP attacks Gordon Brown
after resigning from the Government.

It is hard work to create prosperity
for Britain's hard-working families

that I am interested in, not pompous titles
— *Peter Mandelson on jettisoning the title President of the Board of Trade.*

The more I corrected the aircraft in one direction, the more it continued to go in the opposite direction
— *Louis Bleriot who crashed into a lake moments after take-off trying to repeat his grandfather's 1909 maiden flight across the Channel.*

I am delighted. I would be a funny granny if I was not
— *Mrs David Edelsten on her daughter Melanie Cable-Alexander's baby, fathered by Lord Snowdon.*

I'm completely fed up. It's impossible to continue under conditions where we're all treated like animals
— *World No. 1 cyclist Laurent Jalabert walks out of the Tour de France over the drug abuse row.*

Did he sleep in his helmet? Could he shave? Did he have a bad neck?
— *Curator of the Ancient House Museum in Thetford, Norfolk, after the discovery of papers showing a man trekked 30,000 miles over six years in 1908 wearing an iron mask and pushing a pram for a $100,000 wager he never received.*

Week ending August 8, 1998

This appointment is replacing democracy with patronage
— *Labour MP Dennis Canavan criticises*

appointment of Gus Macdonald as Scottish Industry Minister.

It's a bit like driving across Britain with your head out of the window
— *Richard Rodriguez after spending 1,000 hours on the Big Dipper at Blackpool.*

I can blow up bridges, ski mountains and free-fall from the skies but in my heart I just want to be a woman
— *Sergeant-Major Joe Rushton, who will be the first transsexual in the British Army.*

This is 50 times better than winning the lottery
— *Geoffrey Woods, whose composition was played by the Welsh Guards in honour of the Queen Mother's 95th birthday.*

African Christianity is not far removed from witchcraft
— *A prominent American bishop replying to an African bishop's assertion that homosexuality is "a white man's disease".*

The institution of monarchy is well past its sell-by date — and, indeed, is actually destructive. Without the monarchy we could have an open society, an open constitution
— *Lord Rothermere, proprietor of the Daily Mail.*

Queen Victoria's husband had a ring attached to the end of his crown jewels
— *The Sun highlights royal body-piercing*

precedents after the news of Princess
Anne's daughter Zara's tongue stud.

Farmers must not be left at the
mercy of the sea
– National Farmers' Union replies to
Commons agriculture committee
recommendation that flood-prone land be
abandoned.

Week ending August 15, 1998

It appears that we've had a major
malfunction of the vehicle
– Cape Canaveral commentator as US
rocket carrying a $1 billion satellite
explodes 42 seconds after take-off.

We feel an unbearable regret over
such a use
– Sony on reports that its video cameras
can be used to see through clothing.

A little of what people want is OK as
long as it's on the harmless end of
the spectrum. The more you try to
ban it the more it will grow
– James Ferman, outgoing head of the
British Board of Film Classification, on
pornography.

I know many of the mink are going
to die but at least they will have had
a taste of freedom
– Animal Liberation Front after releasing
6,000 animals from a fur farm in
Hampshire.

This was the hottest July in the
history of the world
– American Vice-President Al Gore

announces the highest average monthly
temperature since records began in 1880.

I've cried for Britain. My eyes got so
bad I found myself thinking only
surgery could sort them out
– Television presenter Anthea Turner,
photographed wearing only a snake,
describes her recent emotional upheavals.

This is Tiggs . . . I won't be here for
yonks and yonks and yonks
– Message on Tiggy Legge-Bourke's
answerphone.

In place of a whining victim culture
we have the heroic selflessness of
figures such as Angus Fraser and
Michael Atherton, who would not
have been out of place at Dunkirk
– The Daily Mail celebrates England's
cricketing victory against South Africa.

If living next to a police station
doesn't make a difference, God
knows what will
– Victim of six burglaries.

Week ending August 22, 1998

It constituted a critical lapse in
judgment and a personal failure on
my part for which I am solely and
completely responsible
– President Clinton on his "inappropriate"
relationship with Monica Lewinsky.

It was a commercial target. We offer
our apologies to the civilians
– The Real IRA says sorry for the
Omagh bomb.

In the 1960s it was almost compulsory to take vodka
— *Ikea boss Ingvar Kamprad dates his 30-year alcohol problem to doing business in Poland.*

He left us as he came to us, fired with enthusiasm
— *Headmaster's reference for a teacher he dismissed, quoted in a letter to* The Times.

I hear it's some sort of a party
— *American baritone Thomas Hampson, on being asked to sing "Rule Britannia" at the Last Night of the Proms.*

At 70, I'm in fine fettle for my age, sleep like a babe and feel around 12. The secret? Lots of meat, drink and cigarettes and not giving in to things
— *Jennifer Paterson, one of the Two Fat Ladies cooks.*

Some motorists view their cars as an extension to their sexuality and driving develops into a complicated mating ritual
— *Conrad King, the RAC's consultant psychologist, on "road lust".*

I felt a bit scared because I hadn't really done this before
— *Matthew Williams, 10, who found toddler Liam Evans alone near the wreckage of his dead grandfather's car.*

As you stir it, it feels thin, but when you stop stirring, it feels thick. So it is liquid enough to cover your chips, but thick enough to stick on the chip and not drip on your trousers

— *Professor Laurie Hall, of Cambridge University, on tomato ketchup.*

Week ending August 29, 1998

Rumours of Ralph Fiennes's acting ability are wildly exaggerated. He is as asexual as an adenoid
— *Feminist writer Camille Paglia.*

Far from going together like a horse and carriage, love and marriage have been in opposition for years
— *Bel Mooney, who is married to television inquisitor Jonathan Dimbleby.*

The Latin American carnival of grief has dwindled and become, as religions tend to become, the preserve of children, homosexuals and lonely housewives. The majority will allow her to sink into oblivion
— *A. N. Wilson assesses the nation's attitude to Diana, Princess of Wales.*

The British public will not stand for a suffering hamster
— Evening Standard *editorial deplores a Levi's advert featuring the death of a hamster.*

I'm in love with Trevor McDonald
— *Lauren Booth, half-sister of Cherie Blair.*

Even God has become female. God is no longer the bearded patriarch in the sky. He has had a sex change and turned into Mother Nature
— *Fay Weldon on the "feminisation" of society.*

If couples need Viagra, they shouldn't be getting married in the first place
– *William Oddie, editor of* The Catholic Herald.

I hope that after my Lord Chancellorship, people will say I am a people's Lord Chancellor
– *Lord Irvine of Lairg.*

I always feel that the hole is too small ▼
– *Golfer Mark James when asked how his sport could be improved.*

Week ending September 5, 1998

Tony Blair is only Bill Clinton with his zip done up
– *Former Tory MP Neil Hamilton.*

Because someone has to tell the truth to the people

– *Bill Clinton on why he visited Moscow.*

Sinn Fein believe the violence we have seen must be for all of us now a thing of the past, over, done with and gone
– *Sinn Fein president Gerry Adams.*

I like being someone else for two hours
– *Emma Noble, James Major's fiancée, when asked why she wanted to act.*

We saw seats, suitcases, clothing and people – bodies. We saw no survivors
– *Rescue worker commenting on Swissair flight which crashed off Canada killing 229 people.*

I don't want to hear about ironing. I don't want to smell the iron. Why? I regard it as a badge of servitude
– *Novelist Maeve Binchy.*

I flushed my angelfish down the loo in the belief they were dead, but they might only have been poorly. It's a terrible thing to have on your conscience
– *Fay Weldon.*

People still haven't gotten over the Beatles yet, which is amazing to me. It's like, God, it's so pathetic
– *Sean Lennon, son of John.*

She would have known that constant reminders of her death can create nothing but pain to those she has left behind
– *Princes William and Harry on their late mother.*

We are exhorted to remember Diana. Have we been allowed to forget her?
– *Letter to* The Daily Telegraph.

Week ending September 12, 1998

It's too strong to call it an obsessive compulsive disorder
– *Psychologist Oliver James on Tony Blair's love of pop music.*

I am sure Michael Owen won't be surprised to learn that he is a gay heart-throb
– *Boy George.*

I love football and am a great supporter of those who broadcast it
– *Peter Mandelson.*

Many imported nurses are entirely delightful, but few speak much

English. Imported doctors have the same difficulty. Bit by bit, all conversations about health will have to be conducted in pidgin English with sign language
– *Auberon Waugh.*

One could never make love to a woman with a glottal stop
– *Brian Sewell.*

If we lose this ballot, we could be out of office for a generation
– *Tory leader William Hague on the snap poll he is calling on the single currency.*

I don't think I am writing books for people too stupid to wear their baseball caps the right way round
– *Terry Pratchett, bestselling author.*

I eat lamb and will continue to. I have a French mother, and food comes first and risk afterwards
– *Lord Sainsbury, Minister for Science.*

The report contains substantial and credible information that may constitute grounds for impeaching the President
– *Spokesman for Kenneth Starr, the independent investigating counsel.*

We should change the name of the town
– *Citizen of Clinton, North Carolina.*

We have got nothing to go on
– *Policeman Nigel Boynton reporting on the theft of 30 potties from a Harrogate shop.*

Week ending September 19, 1998

A company director who takes a pay rise of £50,000 when the rest of the workforce is getting a few hundred is not part of some general trend. He is a greedy bastard
– *John Edmonds, president of the TUC.*

Gentlemen are not supposed to tell the truth about their sex lives, nor are ladies, for that matter. Of course Clinton lied – as would anybody in his position
– *Gore Vidal.*

The answer to speeding on country roads is simple: don't maintain them to our ridiculously high standards. There's nothing like potholes to slow up irresponsible drivers
– *Letter in* The Times.

Covent Garden is a place where businessmen dump their wives in order to keep them quiet
– *Jonathan Miller.*

I don't really think the NHS should be financing people waving their potency at a disco
– *Health Secretary Frank Dobson, on making Viagra available on the National Health Service.*

The Institute of Directors should take their heads out of the pig trough long enough to take a look at the real world
– *Ken Livingstone.*

Week ending September 26, 1998

For people who have risen to the top of their professions by the gift of the gab, even the randier MPs' seduction routines would look clumsy in a Gateshead nightclub
– *Susannah Jowitt, former Commons researcher.*

If you sack politicians for having affairs, then we are going to have a depleted Commons
– *Labour MP Oona King.*

Kenneth Starr, now unveiled as America's No. 1 pornographer, is far more widely despised than Mr Clinton
– *Arthur Schlesinger, historian of the American presidency.*

It's a common misapprehension that all he does is play golf
– *Buckingham Palace spokesman, commenting on the Duke of York.*

Lord, make my words sweet and reasonable; some day I may have to eat them
– *Paddy Ashdown.*

Does anyone sane really give a hoot about the Queen's head on a bank note?
– *Scotsman overheard on Brighton-London train.*

We get lots of sponsorship for otters

and red squirrels, but none for the narrow-headed ant
— *Dr Simon Lyster, director-general of the Wildlife Trust.*

Week ending October 3, 1998

A TV researcher asked me what I made of Cool Britannia. I told him that to me it meant old people with hypothermia
— *Tony Benn.*

There'll be no need for wind farms once the Welsh Assembly gets going. There will be enough hot air to keep the Principality lit up night and day
— *Letter to* The Times.

A newspaper poll found that fewer than one in 20 could explain the Third Way. Some thought it was a religious cult, others a sexual position, and one man asked if it was a plan to widen the M25
— *Keith Waterhouse.*

We don't want to change the House of Lords to a House of Clones. We want to see a chamber that has the maverick, the loose cannon, the independent and the bloody-minded
— *Labour MP Andrew Mackinlay.*

Sexual charisma is not high among Tory leaders
— *Conservative MP Alan Clark.*

Many people around me smoked pot, but I'm a puritan in cavalier's clothing and was never tempted
— *Sir Roy Strong.*

I will eat less
— *Yuri Luzhkov, the portly mayor of Moscow, on how he would deal with expected food shortages this winter.*

Week ending October 10, 1998

Spirituality is like putting petrol in a car. To get the soul going, you have to give it light and energy, and that's spirit
— *The Duchess of York.*

What ho, Elizabeth R
— *The Queen Mother's greeting to a society honouring P. G. Wodehouse.*

The party isn't being run by big beasts in the jungle any more. It belongs to the members
— *William Hague.*

It's exciting for me to see William Hague, as I am the only person in the country who admires his looks
— *TV presenter Clive Anderson.*

It felt different for about three weeks. It was fantastic. It was so romantic, a feeling of being not owned but possessed, which I had never had before. And it's not to be sneezed at
— *Actress Helen Mirren on married life.*

I do not enjoy being famous. The biggest gift in life is anonymity
— *TV gardener Alan Titchmarsh.*

To have a boring machine named after me has always been my dream. It's better than sex

– Actress Maureen Lipman, whose name has been given to a tunnelling machine working on a sewage treatment plant.

me in it really needs its head examined
– The seventh Earl of Onslow.

Week ending October 17, 1998

I believe agriculture has lost its soul. Organic farming can put its soul back
– The Prince of Wales.

Who is going to look after the hills?
– Scottish borders farmer on the shortage of hill farmers.

Don't be cool. It's very boring
– Stephen Fry's advice to pupils at his old school, Uppingham.

Where did you say you was the king of, mate?
– BBC security man to former King Constantine of Greece at London Television Centre.

You don't have to go to Oxford and Eton to get yourself a nice house
– Footballing hard man Vinnie Jones.

Absolutely, I'll find some excuse
– Helen Mirren when asked if she would be stripping off in her role as Cleopatra.

I am going to miss cheese-and-onion crisps and Irn-Bru
– Iraqi child in a "thank-you" letter to Tony Blair before leaving for home after being treated in Britain for cancer.

I have been in favour of Lords reform almost since I have been there, because any House which has

Week ending October 24, 1998

What is Shredded Wheat? Is it a television presenter?
– French judge during Geoffrey Boycott's trial in Grasse.

Everybody's talking French. I don't understand
– Geoffrey Boycott during the court case.

History is too important to be left to historians
– Author and columnist Robert Harris.

Please don't torture me any longer, sir, I made a mistake. Other fighters have made more
– Boxer Mike Tyson appealing, successfully, for his licence to be returned.

A cause for celebration
– Joan Jara, wife of singer Victor Jara, one of thousands killed in Chile under Pinochet, on his arrest in London.

General Pinochet must be allowed to return to his country forthwith
– Margaret Thatcher.

Over the years many people have started articles by Ms Toynbee; few ever finish them
– Right-wing columnist Bruce Anderson, after left-wing columnist Toynbee threw a glass of wine over him.

Yes, I suppose in a sense I am
— *Bank of England Governor Eddie George asked if he is saying that unemployment in the North East is an acceptable price to pay for curbing inflation in the South.*

Week ending October 31, 1998

Does this mean that men like Saddam Hussein and Slobodan Milosevic are safe to swan about the globe knowing that legally they are untouchable?
— *Query after High Court ruling on General Pinochet's legal status.*

I will be sad if I either look up or down after my death and don't see my son fast asleep on the same benches on which I have slept
— *Lord Onslow opposes Labour reforms for the House of Lords.*

People seem to think we are a lot of effete old codgers, sleeping on the red benches and waking only to cause the Government unnecessary problems
— *Lord Feldman of Frognal.*

Isn't it enough to say that as a member of the Cabinet I am accepting that I was guilty of an error of judgment?
— *Welsh Secretary Ron Davies in his resignation letter.*

There are only so many times you can ask a question. There are no salient facts in our possession that are not in yours
— *No. 10 on Ron Davies's actions on Clapham Common.*

I think Peter Mandelson is certainly gay
— *Matthew Parris.*

I will not be availing myself of this service
— *Ann Widdecombe on Parliament's in-house masseuse.*

Week ending November 7, 1998

I gave up smoking at the age of 11. I had one or two strong ones behind the chicken run at school
— *The Prince of Wales.*

We are what we are. We are all different, the products of our genes and our experiences
— *Former Welsh Secretary Ron Davies.*

If I were gay and an active politician, I guess that I would make it known for the thoroughly bad reason that I could not stand years of nervous waiting for some ghastly tabloid reporter to come knocking
— *Lord Hattersley.*

We haven't said they're all hopeless, but quite a few of them are
— *Lady Jay on her fellow members of the House of Lords.*

It has been suggested that Lords should be able to wear jeans. If anyone in the Commons wore jeans when I was Speaker, they would wait a year before they were asked to speak
— *Lord Weatherill.*

Why do we need a Poet Laureate at all? We might as well still retain a Court Jester or a Royal Food Taster
— *Keith Waterhouse.*

You learn not to make jokes, otherwise you find the Germans getting it ten minutes after the Swedes
— *Labour MEP Glenys Kinnock on the perils of speaking in the European Parliament.*

Week ending November 14, 1998

The Conservative Establishment has always treated women as nannies, grannies and fannies
— *Tory MP Teresa Gorman.*

I thought he was one of the saddest men I had ever met
— *Royal biographer Penny Junor on the Prince of Wales.*

If Nick Brown had confessed to being a Sunderland supporter, that would really have been it
— *A member of Newcastle Labour Club on the "outed" Agriculture Minister.*

I am far taller and more handsome than I appear on TV
— *Harrods boss Mohammed Al Fayed.*

The British worker is being hammered at home and milked abroad
— *Tory MP John Wilkinson on taxes demanded by Whitehall and Europe.*

He says it's silly because she doesn't need the money

— *Jerry Hall explains Mick Jagger's objections to their daughter Elizabeth, 14, doing modelling stints.*

The actor I really feel close to is Charlie Chaplin
— *Archbishop of Canterbury.*

Are we being run by a gay Mafia?
— The Sun.

Week ending November 21, 1998

In my view stability is a sexy thing
— *Tony Blair.*

You shall not covet your neighbour's donkey
— *General Synod's suggested update of the Commandment "Thou shalt not covet thy neighbour's ass".*

I cannot believe the size of her butt. If she does appear in *Playboy*, it will have to be an extra big edition
— *Joan Collins on Monica Lewinsky.*

The more I think about it the more awful it is
— *Mick Jagger on audiences that want songs the Rolling Stones sang 30 years ago.*

The free market has done more to liberate women than all the political posturing in the feminist movement
— *Teresa Gorman.*

There was no excuse for this kind of behaviour. He was very well-mannered as a child
— *Mother of singer Robert Del Naja who*

swore at the Duchess of York at an awards ceremony.

Geri, how are you?
– Jean-Paul Gaultier confuses the Duchess of York with Ginger Spice at the same ceremony.

It's not a good idea to hang out with politicians
– Comedian Harry Enfield.

Week ending November 28, 1998

I could never be a politician. I couldn't bear to be right all the time
– Peter Ustinov.

It's a human victory, not a political victory. Every torturer should be brought to justice
– Former soldier in Chilean army on Lords decision about General Pinochet.

What makes food such a tyranny for women? A man may in times of crisis hit the bottle (or another person), but he rarely hits the fridge
– Joanna Trollope.

I am a modern woman. I can't be bothered to cook a pie for eight-and-a-half hours
– Ivana Trump.

I can mix a margarita in five seconds
– Actor Michael Fox, 37, jokes about tremors, which are symptoms of his Parkinson's disease.

Ist dies der gefährlichste Mann Europas?
– The Sun asks whether German finance minster Oskar Lafontaine is the most dangerous man in Europe.

Off with their heads. That's what we voted for
– Polly Toynbee on the hereditary peers.

The institution of monarchy is inherently silly
– Lord Hattersley.

The royals are far more human than people give them credit for
– Rory Bremner.

Week ending December 5, 1998

I was sacked for running around like an ill-trained spaniel
– Lord Cranborne.

It's a girl
– Slogan of beer advertisement showing typical Nativity scene, dismissed by the Church of England as "tasteless".

Thank you, where's my cheque?
– Chris Ofili, who uses dung in his paintings, receives the Turner Prize.

Can you reflect on the fact that last Thursday you took part in a two-horse race in the northeast of Scotland and managed to come third?
– Scottish Nationalist leader Alex Salmond asks the Prime Minister about a by-election.

Perhaps we gave our fans too much by winning the double. Once you have eaten caviare, it is difficult to go back to sausage and mash
— *Arsène Wenger, Arsenal manager, on his team's slump.*

If I were to choose a place to live, I would certainly prefer Wolverhampton to Florence
— *Lord Hattersley.*

It is the age-old game of rat and louse
— *Former Tory MP Jerry Hayes on relations between politicians and the press.*

The unanimity rule cannot be maintained
— *German finance minster threatens to impose tax rises which the UK cannot veto.*

Week ending December 12, 1998

Jack Straw has made a correct, courageous and brilliant decision
— *Labour MP Jeremy Corbyn on the Home Secretary's decision to allow Senator Pinochet's extradition to Spain.*

This is a day of dishonour. Justice in England is political
— *Lord Lamont.*

I don't know how much it is because it's krone
— *John Hume on the Nobel Peace Prize he shares with David Trimble.*

Statistically you stand just as good a chance of winning the Lottery if you don't buy a ticket
— *Lottery host Bob Monkhouse.*

I thought of renaming Ben, my ill-trained labrador, as Cranborne. But I could not do it. He is just too loyal
— *Lord Tebbit.*

It's very hard to be in awe of politicians
— *TV presenter Kirsty Wark.*

There is not an anti-English bone in my body. I have forgotten more about English history than most Tory MPs ever learnt
— *Scottish National Party leader Alex Salmond.*

It was very noisy. We had to edit out all the sounds before showing the interview
— *John Simpson on how Colonel Gaddafi frequently broke wind during an interview.*

December 19, 1998

Instead of the inspectors disarming Saddam, Saddam has disarmed the inspectors
— *President Clinton justifying the attack on Iraq.*

There can be no greater responsibility upon a Prime Minister than to ask British servicemen to risk their lives . . . and I feel that responsibility, tonight, profoundly
— *Tony Blair as attack on Iraq was launched.*

It is a terrible slur on a chap to think that a journalist could keep his

mouth shut for more than five minutes on anything of importance
– *Jeremy Deedes, managing director of the* Telegraph Group, *defends* Sunday Telegraph *editor Dominic Lawson after allegations that he worked for MI6.*

I didn't feel I looked very good. I thought, "Oh no, they're going to ask for an autograph."
– *Britt Ekland giving evidence on the street-theft of the Rolex watch from her wrist.*

The police told me I had been seen staggering
– *John Prescott on a hoax phone call reporting him drink-driving.*

I appreciate anything nice that someone says to me
– *Monica Lewinsky on being the toast of the New York party circuit.*

Week ending December 26, 1998

Dear Tony, I can scarcely believe that I am writing this letter to you
– *Opening of Peter Mandelson's letter of resignation.*

Here's a Ramadan present from Chad Rickenberg
– *Message written by US serviceman on 2,000lb bomb before it was dropped on Baghdad.*

This one's for free
– *Abigail Saxon on her third nude circuit at a BBC Religious Affairs Department Christmas party.*

The only sort of agent I could ever be is a free one
– Sunday Telegraph *editor Dominic Lawson denies that he had been a spy.*

When I saw her I just thought, "Go on, Vinnie, my son, seize the day."
– *Vinnie Jones after dancing with Princess Michael of Kent at a charity function.*

The leading symbol of the hagiography of US mercantilism
– *Fidel Castro on Santa Claus.*

Dear boy, I can hardly close the door
– *Alan Clark MP when asked if he had any skeletons in his cupboard.*

The world is crammed with wronged wives with only their grievances to keep them warm
– *Linda McDougall, wife of Labour MP Austin Mitchell.*

Consumer capitalism has eaten up the Church, the state, trade unions, extended families, everywhere that people learn morality
– *Writer Irvine Welsh.*

Two fairly publicity-friendly, controversial, fairly exotic personalities
– *Peter Mandelson on Geoffrey Robinson and himself.*

1999

I'm not as rich as many in the West think. All my money is gone
— *Mikhail Gorbachev who lost his savings in a Russian bank collapse.*

There's a misconception with some people that England players don't care
— *Bowler Dean Headley after England won a Test match in Australia.*

I was absolutely ecstatic. To see your child's TV debut on Christmas day is probably one of the best things that can happen to you after you've had them
— *Mother of twin babies which "act" as little Belle Dingle in* Emmerdale.

It is dangerous but it brings real meaning to living. If society wants to bar mankind from such stimulation, then the whole human species might as well be castrated
— *Solo sailor Sir Robin Knox-Johnston on the Sydney-Hobart yacht race in which six people died.*

To spend it with a seal colony in the Outer Hebrides would be rather gorgeous
— *Joanna Lumley on where she would like to see in the Millennium.*

Saddam Hussein is not fit to have a finger on the nuclear trigger. And once we stop to think, nor is anyone else
— *Michael Foot.*

Very sorry
— *Former Khmer Rouge leader Khieu Samphan apologises for helping to arrange the slaughter of nearly two million Cambodians in 1970s.*

Someone may be dirty and scruffy and yet perfectly honest, or they can look suave and respectable and be a murderer. I am not diverted by looks so I can home in on important things
— *Diane Cram, Britain's first blind JP.*

I think any woman who becomes successful is demonised by the media because they can't possibly be attractive, intelligent, nice and genuine. It's just too scary for a woman to be all these things
— *Actress Emma Noble, engaged to John Major's son James.*

The money and effort Richard Branson has been expending on his balloon would have been better put towards making his trains run on time
— *Letter to* The Times.

I was slightly stunned for a minute. Then I suddenly realised I should

actually answer the question. I said yes, yes please
– *Sophie Rhys-Jones. on Prince Edward's proposal.*

We are the very best of friends, and that's essential. It also helps that we happen to love each other as well very much
– *Prince Edward.*

The days of the dinosaur are gone
– *Scottish Landowners' Federation on proposals to hand land back to the people.*

They have not applied for a leave of absence and it's well known we take a strong line on this
– *Oratory School headmaster on the Blairs' failure to excuse their children from school to finish a holiday in the Seychelles.*

I will be back
– *Peter Mandelson.*

I will either take a large sleeping tablet and sleep through the whole thing, or become a waiter for the night. After all, monks are born to serve
– *Dom Antony Sutch, headmaster of Downside, planning for the Millennium.*

We want people to realise that Jesus is not a meek, mild wimp in a white nightie
– *The Rev Tom Ambrose, of the Church's Advertising Network after unveiling a poster of Jesus modelled on Che Guevara with the slogan "Meek, Mild, As If".*

Week ending January 16, 1999

I am really not motivated by revenge of any description. If I wanted to bring down the world around Robin's ears I would have written it very differently
– *Margaret Cook on her book about former husband Robin Cook.*

Since you are obviously so upset I may as well tell you some other bad news. As you suspected, I've been having an affair
– *Robin Cook to Margaret Cook just after her favourite horse was put down.*

It would have been nice if the Foreign Secretary had had an ethical domestic policy as well
– *Letter to* The Times.

I am not guilty. I am a mujahid [holy warrior]
– *Abu al-Hassan, on trial in Yemen for the kidnap and murder of British holidaymakers.*

I've been on a bird-watching holiday in the rainforest, where it is extremely difficult to shave
– *Kenneth Clarke explains his brief flirtation with facial hair.*

They are uncomfortable, scratchy and of questionable hygiene, even if they no longer provide a home for a variety of tiny animals
– *High Court judge on judicial wigs.*

People always lie about sex – to get sex, during sex, after sex, about sex
– *Larry Flynt defending President Bill Clinton.*

Week ending January 23, 1999

I lived at Eton in the 1950s and know all about life in uncomfortable quarters
– *Jonathan Aitken on prison.*

The crib will always be more important than the Dome
– *Cardinal Hume on Millennium jamborees.*

A lot of closet caravanners in the Parliamentary Labour Party would rather have a caravan in South Wales than a villa in Tuscany
– *Labour MP Tessa Kingham.*

I wouldn't touch an image consultant with a ten-foot barge-pole
– *Ann Widdecombe.*

I always wanted to go at a time when people would say: "Why is he going?" rather than "Why isn't he going?"
– *Paddy Ashdown.*

I don't have any problem with the idea of putting my feet up. More than anything else, I want to do some flower arranging
– *Speaker Betty Boothroyd on her future.*

I bet my ear to a bag of sweets this will be sorted out in three days

– *Former international player Mike Burton during England's one-day expulsion from the five nations' rugby championship.*

Mr Jagger and Ms Hall are not, and never have been, married
– *Mick Jagger's lawyers contest Jerry Hall's petition for divorce.*

The good, brave and honourable soldier that he is
– *Norman Lamont praises Augusto Pinochet.*

Week ending January 30, 1999

My cooking is modern Scottish – if you complain you get headbutted
– *Chris Bradley, chef of a Michelin-starred restaurant near Ludlow.*

My apologies to the citizens of Chipping Sodbury for calling their town Chipping Sudbury last week. Fact is almost always stranger than fiction
– *Stephen Glover in* The Spectator.

I've wanted to be president for a long time and the year 2000 is looking like my opportunity
– *Dan Quayle, former American vice-president.*

I am saving up for my own hospital trolley
– Dr Who *star Tom Baker on becoming a pensioner.*

I'm shocked. My career must have

slipped. This is the first time I've been able to pick up an award
– *Michael Caine at the Golden Globe awards ceremony.*

Extravagant hospitality, gifts and freebies have been part of the culture of the International Olympics Committee for years
– *John Gummer.*

I'm soon going to be reduced to doing farmyard animals
– *Rory Bremner lamenting the departures of Peter Mandelson, Geoffrey Robinson and Paddy Ashdown.*

I was gobsmacked when I seen her. She was stunning
– *Greg Cordell on the bride he was given in a radio station publicity stunt.*

Week ending February 6, 1999

You and I have been physically given two hands and two legs and half-decent brains. Some people have not been born like that for a reason. The karma is working from another lifetime. I have nothing to hide about that. It is not only people with disabilities. What you sow, you have to reap
– *Glenn Hoddle.*

If he said what he was reported to have said in the way he is reported to have said it, then I think that was very wrong
– *Tony Blair asked about Glenn Hoddle in a Richard and Judy interview.*

It made Des O'Connor look like the Spanish Inquisition
– *Richard Littlejohn on Blair's TV interview with Richard and Judy.*

There is a limit to the number of things politicians should poke their noses into
– *William Hague on Blair on Hoddle.*

There have been times this week when I was wondering what dreadful things I must have done in a previous life to end up as the Sports Minister in this one
– *Tony Banks on the Hoddle affair.*

I have started helping old ladies to cross the road, just in case Mr Hoddle is right
– *Letter to* The Daily Telegraph.

Glenn did not cause offence to the disabled, it was the press
– *Eileen Drewery, faith healer.*

Week ending February 13, 1999

We [the Government] have to try to dominate the agenda because good government demands it
– *Tony Blair's spokesman criticises the press.*

JY1 meant he was the big cheese in Jordan
– *Enthusiast explains King Hussein's call sign as a radio ham.*

Someone is not telling the truth. We cannot ascertain what the truth is

– Select committee on arms-to-Sierra Leone affair.

The trouble with fulfilling your ambitions is you think you will be transformed into some sort of archangel and you're not. You still have to wash your socks
– *Louis de Bernieres, author of* Captain Corelli's Mandolin.

The word I used was "bloody", which, where I come from in Yorkshire, is practically the only surviving adjective
– *Maureen Lipman after criticism for swearing on TV.*

They say an actor is only as good as his parts. Well, my parts have done me pretty well, darling
– *Barbara Windsor after being named a top BBC personality.*

It marks the end of a something-for-nothing welfare state
– *Tony Blair on his welfare reform plans.*

I am afraid it is a non-starter. I cannot even use a bicycle pump
– *Dame Judi Dench, when asked whether she uses e-mail.*

Week ending February 20, 1999

It's the worst day for Frinton since the Luftwaffe beat up the town in 1944
– *Secretary of residents' association on the* council vote allowing the Essex resort its first pub.

I was summoned to see Lord Orr-Ewing and told that this was a most grave matter and must never be repeated
– *Catering manager of the House of Lords on what happened when the macaroons ran out.*

I constantly question whether my hair needs cutting, but not if constitutional reform is right
– *Baroness Jay.*

If I do this I will never be a private person again
– *Governor George Bush Jr of Texas on whether to run for the presidency.*

Men are not supposed to have perfect skin. I do like a nice spot here and there
– *Emma Noble.*

I have never at any point in any of my speeches referred to the last war
– *Robin Cook responds to German claims that Britain's Second World War victory remained its "spiritual core".*

I don't operate rationally. I think just like a woman
– *Vacuum cleaner inventor James Dyson.*

My mum cried when I told her. It's the first time I've done something she can tell the neighbours about
– *Pop star Fatboy Slim on his engagement to Zoe Ball.*

Week ending February 27, 1999

I'm still clinging to the hope of justice
— *Neville Lawrence, father of the murdered boy Stephen Lawrence.*

Black people are still dying on the streets and in the back of police vans
— *Doreen Lawrence, Stephen's mother.*

We feel a sense of shame for the incompetence of our investigation and in our dealing with the family. We failed and could and should have done better
— *Sir Paul Condon, commissioner of the Metropolitan Police.*

If you are working class, being an MP is the job your parents always wanted for you. It's clean, indoor work and there is no heavy lifting
— *Diane Abbott MP.*

A man who is slovenly and untidy is considered normal. The woman who is either is a slut or a slommack or a sloven or a slag
— *Germaine Greer.*

People in Soho keep telling me that I should be embarrassed. But the ironic thing is that in Soho everyone's dad is a Tory
— *Harry Enfield on his father joining the Conservative Party.*

We used to have nimbys, but now I am told that we have a newer, even tougher generation known as Bananas: Build Absolutely Nothing Anywhere Near Anything
— *The Prince of Wales.*

We can no longer afford to pretend that the euro does not exist
— *Tony Blair.*

Week ending March 6, 1999

I cannot say why some were left and some were killed . . . there were soldiers doing what they wanted
— *Uganda tour operator Mark Ross.*

We found ourselves alone. I was very nervous and remember thinking, "this is your chance, so you better tell him, otherwise he's not going to know what to do". So I told him I had a crush on him
— *Monica Lewinsky.*

It wasn't that these police officers were lazy, it wasn't that they were corrupt, as the Lawrence family allege, they were just blithering idiots
— *Geoffrey Robertson QC.*

When I was young and irresponsible, I was young and irresponsible
— *Governor George Bush of Texas when asked if he had experimented with drugs.*

It's gay bar culture. They may love mincing around but I'm not going on TV in a shell suit with wet-look hair

– *Tory MP Alan Clark, responding to William Hague's suggestion that his colleagues should look less stuffy.*

Providing beef on the bone is illegal – eating it is not
– *Spokesman for the Ministry of Agriculture.*

There's so much darn porn out there, I never got out of the house
– *Actor Jack Nicholson explaining why he disconnected his home computer from the Internet.*

Week ending March 13, 1999

Being in the public eye, as Monica Lewinsky will be for the rest of her life, is like being the lady with the moustache at the circus. You're a curiosity – and you will never stop being one
– *Christine Keeler.*

I am not in favour of talking posh
– *Dame Beryl Bainbridge after criticising regional accents.*

I do understand some of those feelings which young blacks experience from time to time
– *Black Home Office race relations adviser who has been stopped 44 times by police.*

He didn't know how to tango, but he obviously knew how to dance
– *Argentine dancer on the Prince of Wales's efforts in Buenos Aires.*

Chaos but very interesting
– *Camilla Parker Bowles on Stella McCartney's fashion show in Paris.*

It is extremely frustrating to hear someone else singing snatches of our song but doing it so completely out of tune
– *Paddy Ashdown on the Budget.*

I don't think we have failed, we have just found another way that doesn't work
– *Pilot of the failed round-the-world balloon flight.*

I have considered myself bound to observe the law for the whole of my 66 years
– *Sir Bernard Ingham, after he was bound over to keep the peace by Croydon Magistrates.*

Week ending March 20, 1999

These hard questions I get, I tell you . . . It was actually . . . no . . . you will like this . . . It was when we redrafted the new Clause Four; the first line is: the Labour Party is a democratic socialist party
– *Tony Blair when asked in Parliament whether he was a socialist.*

I go where I am told
– *John Prescott on why he went to the Maldives.*

Maybe I was a little careless
– *European Commissioner Edith Cresson, one of eight Commissioners accused of*

corruption, mismanagement, nepotism and fraud, leading to the resignation of EU President Jacques Santer and all 20 of his Commissioners.

There is something about the British psyche that appeals to me. They have got fire underneath, but on the outside they are reserved. I like that
— *Gwyneth Paltrow.*

When I gave my big speech on the Lords, the longest letter I received was from a lady who wanted to know where I had bought my blouse
— *Baroness Jay.*

Someone who can't see something working in practice without asking whether it would work in theory
— The Economist *defines an economist.*

It will be a small family affair. We will be inviting about 100,000 people and I've got a couple of symphony orchestras on hold
— *Sir Ralph Vyvyan on his eclipse party in Cornwall.*

I can only suggest you drink less
— *Faith healer Eileen Drewery when asked to cure a hangover.*

Week ending March 27, 1999

If you don't understand what worrries me about the expansion of Nato, then why are you working for the BBC?
— *Mikhail Gorbachev puts Jeremy Paxman in his place in a TV interview.*

The potential consequences of military action are serious for Nato forces and for people in the region
— *Tony Blair warns that war with Serbia will cost British lives.*

I was only 18 and there I was kissing Gwyneth. It was absolutely fantastic
— *Actor Daniel Brocklebank who played Juliet to Paltrow's stage Romeo in* Shakespeare in Love.

She's a little shining star and I still try to see her as much as possible
— *Duchess of York on the Queen who bought her a £1.5m mansion.*

Clobba Slobba
— The Sun *goes to war on Slobodan Milosevic.*

When you are in love you cannot organise your body
— *Roberto Benigni on why he climbed over the seats to collect his Best Foreign Film Oscar.*

An MP, convicted of making a false election expenses return, has been ordered to do community service. Isn't that what MPs are supposed to do?
— *Letter to* The Times.

You will forgive me, won't you, my royal gorgeousness?
— *Cilla Black to the Duke of York after introducing him as the Duke of Edinburgh.*

Week ending April 3, 1999

Sorry, we didn't know it was invisible
– *Placards held by Belgraders celebrating
the downing of a Nato Stealth plane.*

They told us they were going to kill
all the men. We cried and begged
them not to, we fell to our knees, we
offered them money. They all just
laughed and shoved their guns in our
faces
– *Albanian refugee.*

For every act of barbarity, every
slaughter of the innocent, Slobodan
Milosevic must be made to pay a
higher and higher price
– *Tony Blair.*

The chances of catching it quickly
are really rather slim. We've got to try
to find it first. We need to establish its
patterns of behaviour
– *RSPCA inspector James Lucas on an
alligator at large in West Bromwich.*

We were never for a moment
suggesting that people who have
racist conversations at dinner should
be prosecuted
– *Sir William Macpherson on his report
into the Stephen Lawrence affair.*

Men might be put off by this, but I
don't shave my legs. I haven't got
really hairy legs and I think spiky
stubble is worse
– *Geri Halliwell.*

Week ending April 10, 1999

There are thousands and thousands
of people on the other side of the
border not being fed, babies being
born, people becoming sick. And if
everyone is in a tizz in London
talking about getting people out it's
irrelevant to the crisis here
– *Clare Short in Macedonia.*

Ethnic cleansing is leading to the
crucifixion of Kosovo. Military
action is recognition that the civilised
world cannot stand by and accept
that evil should triumph
– *Dr George Carey, Archbishop of
Canterbury.*

This must be the first time in history
that a separatist party has deliberately
tried to conceal its sole purpose for
existing from the electorate
– *Donald Dewar on the SNP's election
manifesto.*

Beats the wedding
– *Wayne Sleep recalling what Diana,
Princess of Wales said after they danced
together at the Royal Opera House.*

The bear does not change his spots
– *Tory defence spokesman Lord Burnham
on Russia.*

You do not report daily that the sun
rose in the east. So why report
annually that the National Union of
Teachers is opposed to reform of the
education system
– *Letter to* The Times.

Tacky and amateurish
– *College of Arms on coat of arms commissioned by Posh Spice and David Beckham.*

Week ending April 17, 1999

The earth itself will burn under the occupiers' feet
– *Slobodan Milosevic warns of the consequences of a Nato ground invasion.*

There is something about Liz's running style that is cramped and uneconomical. She surges forward like a horse trying to catch a carrot
– *British marathon record-holder Veronique Marot disparages Liz McColgan's technique.*

Chris Woodhead has been arrogant, overbearing, critical, and had a terrible effect on the teaching profession. He is lying over this affair but he thinks he is above scrutiny
– *Kate Illingworth, who worked with him at the time of his alleged affair with a pupil.*

It would mean a Scottish neverendum
– *Donald Dewar claiming an SNP government would hold referendum after referendum if elected in May.*

It is a far cry from jam and Jerusalem but the result is a tasteful yet revealing calendar which we are all proud of
– *A member of Rylstone and District Women's Institute in North Yorkshire on their new, nude calendar.*

It's an experience you can always look back on
– *Greg Cordell, whose radio-station-arranged marriage fell apart this week.*

The avant-garde has gone to Tesco's
– *David Bailey bemoans dumbed-down Cool Britannia.*

Week ending April 24, 1999

Women can do without man – in running, anyway
– *London marathon winner Joyce Chepchumba.*

That would be difficult
– *Sir Edward Heath at a photocall when Baroness Thatcher said to him "You should be on my right".*

It's not the first time I have died in Coventry
– *Former Fairport Convention violinist Dave Swarbrick after reading his obituary in* The Daily Telegraph.

Our motives were more social than political as it was a good way to meet boys
– *Cherie Blair on why she joined the Labour Party.*

The Beatles are a Shakespeare for the 20th century
– *Helen Reddington, lecturer in commercial music at the University of Westminster.*

When asked to name my favourite

bird I usually name the bar-tailed godwit
— *Kenneth Clarke.*

Success is the only exit strategy I am prepared to consider
— *Tony Blair.*

Conservatism is not, never has been and never will be solely about the free market
— *Peter Lilley.*

The itemised telephone bill ranks up there with suspender belts, Sky Sports channels and *Loaded* magazine as inventions women could do without
— *Novelist Maeve Haran.*

Week ending May 1, 1999

Part of growing up is learning how to control your impulses
— *Hillary Clinton, introducing her husband at a gun-control rally.*

Sam will not enjoy his childhood . . . Sam is being educated not so as to enjoy himself, but so other people will enjoy him
— *Roger Scruton on the upbringing of Samuel Scruton, aged five months.*

To Jill, we will miss you dreadfully. Do sleep well
— *Message from Nick Ross, Jill Dando's fellow* Crimewatch *presenter.*

I'll never feel sad again
— *Singer Mother Bernadette Marie,*

formerly Sinead O'Connor, after being ordained as a Catholic priest.

Never turn down a drink, unless it is of local manufacture
— *George Walden's advice for travelling with the Queen.*

Scotland should be nothing less than equal with all the other nations of the world
— *Sean Connery.*

When the clock strikes midnight on 31/12/99 the White Wolves will begin to howl, & when the Wolves begin to howl, the Wolves begin to hunt. You have been warned. Rule Britannia
— *Neo-Nazi group claims credit for bomb in London.*

We had left our front door open by accident and found six Japanese tourists in our sitting room waiting for a tour
— *Simon Howard, owner of Castle Howard.*

Week ending May 8, 1999

I am very proud of him. He's the underdog who cheated the system
— *Mike Biggs on his father, Great Train Robber Ronnie Biggs.*

Never met any
— *Lord Healey when asked to name the woman epitomising the English rose.*

The man who has been eating the people of Scotland
— *Slip of the tongue by John Prescott referring to Donald Dewar.*

I just want some love in my life
— *Geri Halliwell.*

It's not covered by any of our training programmes
— *Air stewardess Andrea O'Neill, who ran around a BA plane on the runway in her underwear after a bet.*

If David is guilty of these awful acts of violence, then we also totally condemn him
— *Father of David Copeland, accused of the London nail bombs.*

He had no problem with alcohol
— *Glenda Jackson on Oliver Reed.*

Isn't it the case that these are the only people left in the Labour Party with genuine convictions?
— *William Hague, after listing the Labour councillors found guilty of crimes such as fraud.*

We are gearing our programmes at two to eight-year-olds. We feel that nine-year-olds can no longer be considered children
— *Anne Wood, creator of the Teletubbies.*

Week ending May 15, 1999

The Church should be spreading the gospel, not spreading the fat

— *Norman Baker MP on the luxurious lifestyle of bishops.*

My tutor said you have to have at least two degrees before you are allowed to make jokes in writing
— *Ian Hislop, editor of* Private Eye.

There was an error in the targeting process which caused us to attack the wrong building. We are now reviewing this process
— *Nato explains the bombing of the Chinese Embassy in Belgrade.*

It was the right address applied to the wrong building
— *US intelligence on the mistaken bombing.*

Incredibly insular
— *Orange literary prize judge on writing by British female authors.*

Having a British passport would not make much practical difference to me. I might get through UK airports a bit faster, but that's about all
— *Mohammed Al Fayed.*

In caring for a terminally ill patient, a doctor is entitled to give pain-relieving medication which may have the effect of a patient's death
— *Dr David Moor, acquitted of murdering a patient.*

Easily consumable eye-candy that contains no nutrients for the heart or mind
— Variety *magazine reviews* Star Wars *prequel film* The Phantom Menace.

Week ending May 22, 1999

I am desperate if I find there are British press on a foreign visit. I know they'll wreck the thing if they can
— *The Duke of Edinburgh.*

It's a pleasure to be standing up here. It's a pleasure to be standing up
— *George Best after being named Footballer of the Century.*

Nato has just had its best week yet in terms of successful military strikes
— *Robin Cook.*

Half the Beeb is on coke ▼
— *Chris Evans.*

They are just trying to discredit me as much as they can
— *Mohammed Al Fayed denies publishing MI6 names.*

They should drive their trucks to Downing Street if they feel that strongly
— *Tony Turnbull, taxi driver, stuck on M25.*

It would be a very peculiar sort of poet who would be interested in only writing poems for the wedding of Edward and Sophie
— *Andrew Motion, the Poet Laureate.*

I never run for the bus
— *Linford Christie, Olympic runner.*

Will you stop shouting? It is very disturbing to many of us up here who are trying to rest
– *Labour MP Jeremy Corbyn to Tory MP Quentin Davies during an all-night Commons sitting.*

I hope he's not ugly like his dad
– *Vera Gimenez, grandmother of Mick Jagger's newborn lovechild.*

Week ending May 29, 1999

I made an error in judgment which stems from naivety and foolishness
– *Lawrence Dallaglio, England rugby captain who resigned after being exposed by* News of the World *journalists who pretended to be Gillette executives interested in sponsoring inner city rugby.*

I have smoked a lot of marijuana. It hasn't harmed me
– *David Hockney.*

This has ruined my engagement. This was supposed to be the happiest time of my life
– *Sophie Rhys-Jones after a friend sold a topless picture of her to* The Sun.

I wish her and Prince Edward the very best, although I don't expect to be invited to the wedding
– The Sun's *Editor apologises for printing the picture of Miss Rhys-Jones.*

How dare you fob me off. I am not a tourist from a coach
– *Michael Winner to staff at an hotel.*

Incredible humans
– *Alex Ferguson, Manchester United manager, on his players after winning the European Cup.*

This is a strengthened peace implementation force
– *George Robertson, Defence Secretary, on extra troops for Kosovo.*

He was the most married man I have ever met. I might as well have had a crush on Jesus Christ
– *Receptionist Merri Cheyne describing a hotel night with Lenny Henry.*

Ron, there are no honourable gentlemen in this chamber
– *Speaker for the Welsh Assembly calls for informality in proceedings.*

Week ending June 5, 1999

You can't believe how strong the homosexuals are. Scotland could go back to the darkness very easily
– *US evangelist Pat Robertson who was to work for the Bank of Scotland.*

Since bees and the wind don't obey any sort of rules, we shall soon have an unprecedented and unethical situation in which one farmer's crop will contaminate another's against his will
– *The Prince of Wales on GM foods.*

I heard a phenomenal noise and thought it was the last thing I would hear on earth

– Times *journalist Eve-Ann Prentice after being injured by a Nato bomb in Kosovo.*

The prospect that they could wreck their sex lives might just make them stop and think
– *BMA on claims that smoking can make men impotent.*

It has left companies feeling betrayed because they were promised there would be no more changes
– *Federation of Small Businesses on the new telephone codes.*

They have all got personalities
– *Eric Clapton on his guitars, which he is selling.*

The Irish people will go berserk with anger and rage to see this going on and realise that nothing was done for 25 years
– *Father Dennis Haul on the exhuming of the "disappeared" IRA victims.*

Week ending June 12, 1999

I deeply regret the lies I told and the actions I took to mislead a large number of people
– *Jonathan Aitken before being imprisoned.*

He will be for ever remembered for the odium of being an MP who lied and tried to pervert the course of justice
– *Aitken's defence counsel.*

It's to buy a water-sprinkling system for my house in Ibiza
– *Aitken's mother explains why she sold her story to a tabloid.*

I'm frightened that other prisoners will kick him for coughing and keeping them up
– *Victoria, Aitken's daughter.*

I heard shouts but they were more like whoops for joy. People just thought it was part of the fun
– *A survivor of the white-water rafting accident in Austria in which her boyfriend drowned.*

It is a mistaken assumption that when a bride says she will obey it means she is going to be subservient
– *Bishop of Norwich on the decision of Sophie Rhys-Jones to make traditional wedding vows.*

We are concerned to remind broadcasters that 9pm is a watershed, not a waterfall
– *The Broadcasting Standards Commission after an increase in viewers' complaints about sex and violence on television.*

Week ending June 19, 1999

We are very different people. She had her own personality and I have mine
– *Sophie Rhys-Jones denies she is a Princess Diana clone.*

I certainly see it more as a supporting role to Edward rather than rushing

off and forging my own path
– *Sophie Rhys-Jones on joining the Royal Family.*

They spend more on physical preparation than on playing and it's not good for the image of women's tennis
– *Jana Novotna on young female tennis players.*

She's a very bad role model for our teenagers and I hope they will ignore her
– *Archbishop of Manila on Geri Halliwell, UN goodwill ambassador.*

All clowns are a bit sad inside
– *Yvonne Elwood, girlfriend of the late Screaming Lord Sutch.*

Archbishopatdemon.net
– *E-mail address offered to and rejected by the Archbishop of Wales.*

The scale of the criminality is enormous. The number of people who have been murdered is greater than we think by far. It is going to be chilling
– *Senior British official in charge of investigating war crimes in Yugoslavia.*

We do not believe that the best way forward is to give the Russians, and just the Russians, a whole chunk of Kosovo
– *Nato spokesman Jamie Shea.*

Week ending June 26, 1999

To the public at large, choosing between an earldom and a dukedom is irrelevant
– *Palace official on Edward and Sophie's titles.*

We are sorry for the inconvenience
– *London Underground announcing eight-week closure of the Circle Line.*

It's a big win for me
– *Jelena Dokic, 16, after knocking top seed Martina Hingis out of Wimbledon.*

I think that is a bit greedy
– *Tim Henman on women players' requests for the same Wimbledon prize money as men.*

It is pretty extraordinary to go from Birmingham to Berlin
– *Julian Lloyd Webber on Simon Rattle's new post as music director of the Berlin Philharmonic.*

That is what we battle over . . . who is king of being tired
– *Nicole Kidman and Tom Cruise on how tiring their work is.*

I regard myself as at the forefront of the "verbless sentence"
– *News presenter Jon Snow defends the use of English in the media.*

Children need to get into trouble to learn how to get out of trouble
– *The Mental Health Foundation on over-protective parents.*

This has never happened to me before
– *William Waldegrave on being made a
life peer.*

You're left moved with pity for the
terror those people must have felt
– *Robin Cook, shocked by a massacre
site in Pristina.*

Week ending July 3, 1999

Fortunately my passport does not
expire until next year
– *Jack Straw, Home Secretary.*

I wonder what you do when you do
a hostile interview?
– *Henry Kissinger, furious after a grilling
by Jeremy Paxman on Radio 4's* Start
the Week.

Throw us one more orange and we
could make a fruit salad
– *Keanu Reeves's band, Dogstar, booed
off the stage at Glastonbury.*

She couldn't edit a bus ticket
– *Kelvin MacKenzie on Janet Street-
Porter's appointment as editor of the*
Independent on Sunday.

She's so pretty and I'm pretty lucky
– *Michael Douglas on finding love with
young actress Catherine Zeta-Jones.*

I would have liked a little more
partisanship
– *Jim Courier on crowd reactions during
his match with Tim Henman.*

We're depending on you
– *Children's song to politicians at
Stormont.*

He was that invaluable phenomenon,
a safe pair of hands
– *Baroness Jay on the late Viscount
Whitelaw.*

Tony Benn was the moderniser who
went on to become a socialist terror
in the minds of Middle England
– *Ken Livingstone on Tony Benn.*

Week ending July 10, 1999

We don't want spin with a grin. We
don't want guile with a smile
– *Chairman of the British Medical
Association attacking Tony Blair.*

I know I did wrong. I am not proud
of my activities
– *Nick Leeson, released after four years
in a Singapore prison.*

The economics of the madhouse
– *Chief executive of the World Gold
Council on the Government's decision to
sell most of its gold reserves.*

A man among men, a king among
kings
– *The Prince of Wales paying tribute to
King Hussein at a memorial service in St
Paul's Cathedral.*

What about Bloody Wednesday,
Thursday and Friday?
– *Colonel Wilford on the* Today
programme.

Public speaking isn't David's strong point
— *A wedding guest commenting on David Beckham's speech to his bride.*

I can't handle dealing with two things at once
— *The council worker who successfully sued her employers over stress.*

I don't know how I do it. I really don't
— *Pete Sampras after winning the Wimbledon men's singles for a record sixth time.*

Week ending July 17, 1999

I do not believe that the IRA is contemplating an immediate or early destruction of illegal weapons or explosives
— *Ken Maginnis, the Unionists' security spokesman.*

I am a bit numb but upbeat
— *Detective Inspector Ben Bullock, convicted of two out of 28 alleged breaches in the Stephen Lawrence investigation.*

I found it slightly odd for a man with $1 billion cash burning a hole in his pocket to look so worried
— *Diplomat on Conservative Party treasurer Michael Ashcroft.*

I have always believed in the phrase "shy bairns get nowt"
— *Harvard scholarship winner Lara Dixon, 18, from Whitley Bay.*

I wanted to look quite virginal on my wedding day
— *Victoria Adams.*

Agincourt is not a lucky subject for the French
— *Nicole Manuello, French critic, on the first French-language production of* Henry V.

To take sperm from a dead patient is technically possible, but speaking personally I would be outraged
— *Julian Norman-Taylor, fertility specialist.*

We are up to our knees in Fenian blood, surrender or you'll die
— *Allegedly sung by Scotland football manager Craig Brown into a friend's answerphone.*

Week ending July 24, 1999

You don't get any closer to lighting those engines
— *Launch director of the space shuttle* Columbia, *halted six seconds before lift-off.*

Every year I am your guest of honour. Now I'm thinking I'm a guest of dishonour
— *Zimbabwe's President Robert Mugabe declaring his regime to be corrupt at a private lunch for the opening of Parliament.*

I have not had my fill of Ireland
— *Mo Mowlam tells Tony Blair she wants*

*to stay on as Secretary of State for
Northern Ireland.*

I can't believe it. I think I'm going to
cry
*– Paul Lawrie, outsider and first Scot to
win the Open since 1985.*

Where have you gone, John-John?
– Written tribute to JFK Jr.

I'm a kind of working-class guy in
my heart
– John Prescott.

It's nice when the law gives
something back to poor people
*– Ian Ames, given the deeds to the house
he has squatted in for 15 years.*

The English – in England – are among
the most tolerant bigots on earth
*– Introduction to a new Lonely Planet
British Phrasebook.*

We've never had so many visitors
going "wow, wow" before
*– The manager of Kenwood House,
London, which featured in the film*
Notting Hill.

No flowers please, just caviare
*– "Fat Lady" Jennifer Paterson from her
hospital bed.*

Week ending July 31, 1999

It's whether we want democratic
government or anarchy
– Farmer whose GM crops were uprooted.

Hurry up, not all of us have as much
time as you
*– An 82-year-old woman interrupts Tony
Blair in the House of Commons.*

They are stifling creativity and
depriving children of their right to
childhood
*– Statement about exams by a teacher at
a conference.*

It would be much easier if you could
just lock them up
– Council leader on teenagers.

Not an hour goes by when that crash
is not in the forefront of my mind
– Survivor of Southall train.

I'm Superman
– John Prescott.

I don't think he's reshuffling me
– Cherie Blair.

I don't respond to sound bites
– Helen Liddell, Transport Minister.

Surgeons can at least bury a mistake.
Architects merely suggest that you
can grow a vine over it
– Lord Palumbo.

Why is the Government so reluctant
to use capital letters in its annual
report? This may satisfy the modern
design brief but it will not help
achieve better literacy
– Lib-Dem MP Tom Brake.

Woodstock is supposed to be the spirit of love. This isn't love
– *A visitor to the Woodstock festival, which was marred by violence.*

Week ending August 7, 1999

I don't see why he can't mix with the rest of us
– *Local resident on the closure of five miles of Tuscan beach for the Blairs' exclusive use.*

For goodness' sake, don't let mummy have another drink
– *The Queen's instruction to a pageboy according to a new biography of the Queen Mother.*

I cannot recommend that you travel at peak times
– *Thameslink advice to a pregnant woman who complained about being forced to stand on its trains.*

I was beginning to get a little stale
– *Sports presenter Desmond Lynam, leaving the BBC for ITV.*

A hard dog to keep on the porch
– *Hillary Clinton on her husband in* Talk *magazine.*

I suppose I shall be at my desk
– *Philosopher Roger Scruton on where he will be during the eclipse.*

Week ending August 14, 1999

It's a bit early for my first crisis, surely?

– *Charles Kennedy, the new Liberal Democrat leader, on reports of unrest in the ranks.*

Advance to Go. Collect £2,631,784 and scarper
– *Birthday party invitations from Ronnie Biggs of the Great Train Robbery.*

He was very brave when she was not in the room
– *A senior Tory on John Major's relationship with Margaret Thatcher.*

In retrospect her behaviour was intolerable. I hope none of my successors is treated in that way
– *Major on Thatcher.*

Our children deserve more than bugs and domes
– *The Scripture Union on a survey in which few children linked the Millennium with Jesus.*

It looks as if it was put in by an Indian
– *Prince Philip on an old-fashioned fuse box in an Edinburgh factory.*

It was very quiet afterwards as no one had anything to talk about
– *Concorde travellers demanding their money back because they did not see the eclipse from the plane.*

I feel like crying. That was very emotional
– *An eclipse watcher.*

Evolution has been removed
– *Kansas Board of Education after dropping Charles Darwin's theory of evolution from its curriculums.*

Week ending August 21, 1999

I sit in Tony's room, in Daddy Bear's chair
– *Deputy Prime Minister John Prescott, on running the country in the absence of the Prime Minister.*

So much of our seed this year has been sown in tears
– *A mourner marking the first anniversary of the Real IRA bomb attack in Omagh.*

Peter's fall from grace is complete. The poor man's now living on a bus route
– *A former neighbour of Peter Mandelson.*

I think it's very tough for teenage girls who look sexy before they feel sexy
– *Elizabeth Hurley.*

We can't believe our luck. She is a superstar in America. They particularly love her in Texas
– *Cambridge University development director on Lady Thatcher.*

Week ending August 28, 1999

I was OK until they said "Women and children at the front". It just reminded me of the *Titanic*
– *Passenger on the cruise ship* Norwegian Dream *after its collision.*

I don't understand what all the fuss is about.
– *Wayne Jackson, who dumped his 18-month-old daughter at a police station so he could catch a flight to Spain.*

I was playing with my truck. Then I fell
– *Four-year-old Ismail Cimen, found alive six days after a Turkish earthquake.*

It's a complete joke. What do I put down? My inside leg measurement? My shoe size, number of brain cells?
– *Lord Mancroft on peers being given 75 words to justify remaining in the House of Lords.*

In my parish, one officer covers 260 square miles. All a robber has to do is watch him drive past, wait ten minutes and go ahead
– *Parish councillor on rural crime.*

I couldn't remember my name
– *Bill Clinton on meeting Hillary.*

We've got the worst team in the world
– *Spectators' chant after England cricketers were beaten by New Zealand.*

Week ending September 4, 1999

It's not a question about selling sheep to fund a nice new sheep-shed or make improvements on the farm. In many cases we are talking about funding next week's grocery bill
– *President of the National Farmers' Union on Britain's agricultural crisis.*

I broke the golden rule in chess: never underestimate your opponent
– *John Nunn, the grandmaster defeated by an eight-year-old prodigy.*

I think he was maybe a bit embarrassed
– *David Howell, the eight-year-old who beat him.*

You have got to understand. I am a man with a mission
– *Tony Blair.*

The best example of the use of bosom as a theatrical prop since Barbara Windsor
– The Times *on Ann Widdecombe.*

We are committed to protecting your privacy and developing technology that gives you the most powerful, safe online experience
– *Microsoft, whose free e-mail service was penetrated by hackers.*

Week ending September 11, 1999

I had some homosexual experiences as a young person
– *Michael Portillo.*

He's so dolly and fancy. You need someone a bit trendy and jolly around here
– *Chelsea pensioner on the prospect of Portillo as Conservative candidate.*

Politics is poorer and the world duller with his passing
– *Margaret Thatcher on the late Alan Clark.*

It's hell here and I want to cry out to everyone to save us, but nobody seems to be listening
– *Nun caught in the East Timor civil war.*

You must not, you cannot impose morality
– *Archbishop of Canterbury to Tony Blair.*

It's bland, it's vaguely Labour, like Tony Blair
– *Poet Robert Nye on Andrew Motion's poem to the TUC.*

It used to be the kids that kept me awake at night, now it's the job
– *Tony Blair.*

We are getting away from the leather sandals and lentils approach
– *Sainsbury's on launching organic gin and tonic.*

Week ending September 18, 1999

Oh dear, this is all so different from my quiet little life
– *Melita Norwood to journalists after being exposed as a KGB agent.*

He's not as good looking as me
– *Liam Gallagher on his son Lennon.*

I would never, ever support Archer, dead or alive
– *Steven Norris on Lord Archer, his rival to become Lord Mayor of London.*

I watch my children and Cherie surfing the net and feel a sense of humiliation
– *Tony Blair.*

Good evening. I had a feeling that we'd be meeting again
– *Des Lynam in his first ITV appearance.*

We are not going to push it in people's faces
– *Conservative Future on its new slogan, "cfuk".*

The only bright thing is that not everybody reads *The Daily Telegraph*
– *Colin Dexter on the newspaper which revealed how Inspector Morse dies.*

I don't know where their ethical foreign policy stands now, it seems to have disappeared altogether
– *William Hague on the Government's subsidising the sale of war planes to Indonesia.*

Week ending September 25, 1999

It must be in the Russian character – to run somebody into the mud and then laud them to high heavens after a tragedy strikes
– *A spokesman for Mikhail Gorbachev on the late Raisa Gorbachev.*

We are prepared for the worst but hope for the best
– *Head of the British contingent of the peacekeeping force in Dili, East Timor.*

Basically there is a deadline. It is a thousand years before there will be another one like it
– *Union official on the striking electricians working on Millennium projects.*

I bet you wouldn't have done that if I was staying
– *Paddy Ashdown on an ovation for his farewell speech to the Liberal Democrats.*

They are among the most stigmatised and demonised groups in society
– *Children's Rights Office on under-16s not allowed in the Millennium Dome without an adult.*

For 50 years we have been trained to fight off a Chinese invasion but this has come as a surprise
– *Taiwan clerk on the earthquake which killed thousands.*

Yes, I touched her, but only after she'd touched the most private parts of me
– *Diana Ross, after an airport security search.*

Week ending October 2, 1999

Where do these androids come from?
– *Tony Booth, Tony Blair's father-in-law, on Labour Party officials.*

The lifestyle and morality of Islington are fine, but we don't want them imposed on rural Exmoor
– *Lady Mallalieu.*

We were bleeding to death and all we were doing was talking
– *Norman Lamont writing about Black Wednesday in his memoirs.*

There were security reasons and my wife does not like to have her hair

blown about. Any more stupid questions?
– John Prescott on why he took a chauffer-driven trip to the Labour conference.

With all thse people down here demonstrating, there's not a safer day to be a fox
– Tony Blair on the 16,000 pro-hunting demonstrators in Bournemouth.

My friends! The class war is over
– Tony Blair to the Labour Party.

We're becoming Spice Women now
– Mel C on her new image.

I made a mistake
– Train driver giving evidence at the Southall rail crash enquiry.

I think it considerate of me to have taken on the disease, thus protecting the remaining 99,999 Screen Actors' Guild members from this fate.
– Dudley Moore on his brain disease which strikes only one in 100,000 people.

Week ending October 9, 1999

I never saw her face but I will never forget that hour I held her hand
– A paramedic at the Paddington train crash.

I do not want to talk about it in front of the wife and children
– David Machin, who allegedly had sex with a stranger in a plane.

An Englishman's home is his castle but if he is a tenant he remains in his home only so far as the Rent Acts allow
– Judge Cowell to Gladys Stone on her eviction from her Mayfair apartment.

I was told there were three ways to open a speech: a joke, a quotation and a third way. Well, whatever the third way is I decided I wanted nothing to do with it
– Robert Reed, 16, speaking at the Conservative Party conference.

In my lifetime all our problems have come from mainland Europe and the solutions have come from the English-speaking nations of the world
– Margaret Thatcher at the Conservative conference.

I really don't mind doing Monty Python, providing none of the others are around
– Eric Idle on the new sketches marking the 30th anniversary of Monty Python.

Seduction is rough and ready rather than loving, requiring considerable amounts of alcoholic encouragement in the preliminary stages
– David Ross in his book Xenophobe's Guide to the Scots.

Week ending October 16, 1999

I just don't think this is a way to behave
– Chris Patten on reports that Michael Heseltine was pelted with cocktail

sausages and peanuts at the Conservative Party conference.

I've always adored him, but he doesn't have time for me
– Sarah Ferguson on the Prince of Wales.

It might not have been perfect in every last dot and comma – and whose is?
– Peter Mandelson on his mortgage application form.

One has the impression that the teaching of history in this country stops at 1945
– Gebhardt von Moltke, outgoing German ambassador to Great Britain.

The real denial of our history would be to retreat into isolation from the continent of Europe of which we are part and whose history we have so intimately shaped
– Tony Blair

I am a drug addict, not a paedophile
– Tara Palmer-Tomkinson denies that she has slept with Prince William.

I've never heard of David Hockney
– Amanda Gresham who nearly threw away faxed drawings by the artist which she sold for £11,000.

The books have a tone of death, hate, lack of respect and sheer evil
– South Carolina woman, one of many American parents calling for the Harry Potter books to be banned.

Week ending October 23, 1999

An object with powerful metaphorical resonance
– The Tate explains Tracey Emin's soiled bed, shortlisted for the Turner Prize.

What was he meant to say? You bounder! You cad! Meet me at dawn with pistols
– James Hewitt, former lover of the Princess of Wales, on Prince Charles.

Single women tend to have much more developed and intense social networks and are involved in a wide range of social and other activities
– Professor Richard Scase on why women fare better when living alone.

It is a very difficult assignment
– BBC insider on relaunching Crimewatch with a replacement for murdered presenter Jill Dando.

Next year there will be even fewer clothes
– Shropshire hunt on the success of a calendar with pictures of nude huntsmen and women.

Norway! Norway isn't even in the European Union
– Tony Blair after William Hague said Norway shared the Tory position on Europe.

I don't know anything about music. I've done it all through acting
– Meatloaf, the rock star, reveals the secret of his success.

He's a very good driver
– *Rodney Atkinson after his brother Rowan crashed his £650,000 sports car.*

England is an island. It is easier to blockade than the Continent
– *French farmers' leader explains a demonstration in Calais.*

I hope that will put an end to it
– *Dowager Countess Lucan on her husband Lord Lucan being officially declared dead.*

This bill, drafted in Brussels, is treason. What we are witnessing is the abolition of Britain. Before us lies the wasteland. No Queen, no culture, no sovereignty, no freedom
– *Earl of Burford protests as hereditary peers vote themselves out in the House of Lords.*

It's just not done for a man to touch another man, unless he's just scored a goal on the football pitch
– *Body language expert Allan Pease who claims touch and other "non-verbal communcations" are key to efficient workplaces.*

We just want to show how spontaneous art is superior to the institutionalised art which dominates the Turner Prize
– *Performance artists who jumped on Tracey Emin's bed exhibited in the Tate Gallery.*

You are on the front page of the paper. You have got lots of publicity. Come down now

– *Negotiator trying to persuade protestors to descend from the Millennium wheel.*

Week ending November 6, 1999

I rang the police, but more for their benefit than ours
– *Egon Ronay after he and his wife were mugged in London.*

The vast majority of the British public and Parliament are against foxhunting and the heir to the throne appears to be putting two fingers up to them
– *Mike Foster, Labour MP.*

They are good company. I went to a dinner party the other night and four officers followed me in. the party ended up bigger than the host was expecting
– *Simon Hughes MP on his police guards, after he received death threats for encouraging trial witnesses to give evidence.*

When I was told that ladies were not allowed to wear trousers I thought it was a joke; it seemed so outdated
– *Judy Owen, who resigned after being told she had to wear a skirt in her job at the Professional Golfers Association.*

I'm a nervous wreck
– *Elizabeth Kirk, aged ten, after helping deliver her baby sister.*

Perhaps Tommy Archer will succeed in getting through to them
– *Friends of the Earth on the Government, after the radio character was*

found not guilty of damaging a genetically modified crop.

Week ending November 13, 1999

On Monday you gave the French the Third Way and today they have given you two fingers
– William Hague taunts Tony Blair.

Your majesty, everyone wants a pound of your flesh
– Nelson Mandela to the Queen on her tour of South Africa.

Their deaths were due, at least in part, to unusual weather
– US researchers on how Captain Scott and his team died in the Antarctic.

It has been the perfect divorce
– Jerry Hall on her separation from Mick Jagger.

I was meant to have children. I loved them so much
– Sally Clark, found guilty of murdering her two babies.

The time has come for them to be allowed to participate
– Royal British Legion on inviting the Women's Land Army to its Remembrance Day march at the Cenotaph.

The girls are obviously very annoyed
– Friend of pop band Steps whose male members are paid much more than the girls.

I demanded his resignation and six months later he was gone

– Harry Enfield on a drunken entreaty to Tony Blair at a No 10 party to sack Peter Mandelson.

I am a big softie
– Weatherman Bill Giles denies he is a bully after allegations of high-handed behaviour by colleagues.

Week ending November 20, 1999

The IRA statement is pretty meaningless. There is no timetable, no declaration that the so-called war is over, absolutely no guarantee that decommissioning will ever happen
– David Trimble, Ulster Unionist leader, responds to the IRA on power-sharing before arms talks.

We didn't play well. We just couldn't get going at all
– Kevin Keegan after England lost to Scotland but scraped into the Euro 2000 finals on aggregate.

It is a mess and the sooner it is sorted out, the better
– Frank Dobson on Labour's selection process for Mayor of London candidate.

Horny, but not porny or corny
– Julie Clive, producer of this year's Miss World competition.

The Koran and the Bible say it will be like this. The world will end with earthquakes and floods
– Mustafa Tuncer surveying the ruins of his home town in Turkey after an earthquake.

She looked around squillions of houses and drove everyone nuts. Eventually agents were saying: "God, not her again"
– *Unnamed estate agent, employed by Madonna to find her a house in London.*

It is a complete waste of money. It is architecturally awful and a boring building
– *Sir Jocelyn Stevens, chairman of English Heritage, describing the Millennium Dome.*

Week ending November 27, 1999

In future when he hears the sound of crying next door it won't be the Chancellor wanting his job
– *William Hague commenting on the Blairs' new baby.*

To be honest, the Duke of Windsor was an extremely dull man. Noël said he even danced a boring Charleston, which is no mean feat
– *Graham Payn, recalling life with his lover, friend and companion Noël Coward.*

Let MI5 and MI6 sue me. Let Prince Philip sue me . . . they killed my son
– *Mohammed Al Fayed responding to cross-examination at the High Court.*

I will not tolerate behviour like this in my party. This is the end of politics for Jeffrey Archer
– *William Hague's reaction to the news that Archer had asked a friend to lie in his 1987 libel case against the Daily Star.*

People keep saying: "Are you still doing this or that?" implying it's bloody time I gave up.
– *The Duke of Edinburgh, aged 78, talking about old age and retirement in a magazine interview.*

Stop playing silly games with this generation and the next
– *David Trimble telling Gerry Adams not to stall over arms decommissioning.*

Week ending December 4, 1999

We assume that he must have difficulties or troubles and, painful though it all is, and difficult, frightening and shocking, it is important to pray for his family
– *Father Agley speaking of attacker Eden Strong at a service after the random stabbing in his church.*

There has never been a golden age of the family
– *Jack Straw, Home Secretary.*

When you are 90 and the other person is 41 you don't marry for sex. You may think about it but that is all
– *Ian Patey on marrying his new wife Monica, who is nearly 50 years his junior.*

As a friend I love him and I just ignore anyone who makes comments about it
– *Monica Patey on marrying Ian.*

I think that, where possible, there should be bus lanes on every road

inside the Circle Line to get central London moving. How much would it cost? I don't have a clue. I've only got one researcher
— *Frank Dobson on London's traffic congestion.*

I wouldn't say that he was an angel, but he is basically a good man
— *Alison Bozek, former secretary of Mohammed Al Fayed, on her former employer as she testifies that she witnessed large sums of money being addressed to Neil Hamilton.*

Week ending December 11, 1999

Of all the trees in the world the densest is the redwood
— *John Prescott, Deputy Prime Minister, on criticism from John Redwood.*

My private life has been more speculated on, misrepresented and intruded into than most politicians
— *Steven Norris, would-be London mayor.*

I've never suggested that my steward-ship of this department was perfect
— *Jack Straw, Home Secretary*

I don't regret it
— *James Suton, 13, on fathering twin girls.*

There's been no surgery, no drugs. I had 10,000 people praying for me and my cancer vanished
— *Dr Mary Self, after being diagnosed with terminal bone cancer.*

Many people will find it deeply offensive
— *Lord Alton on a statue of Diana, Princess of Wales as the Virgin Mary.*

At the moment we are calling her Jane.com
— *Emma Thompson, the actress, on her newborn daughter.*

If you feel depressed or let down, my advice is to roast a chicken
— *Delia Smith.*

At this moment in time, what happens here today and changes as we go along, that is part of life's learning and part of your inner beliefs
— *Glenn Hoddle statement which won a booby prize from the Plain English Campaign.*

Week ending December 18, 1999

Revenge of the blue-rinse brigade
— *Steven Norris, briefly dropped as mayoral candidate.*

Democracy is sometimes untidy
— *Michael Ancram on Tory confusion about mayoral candidates.*

It's ripping off the fans
— *Spice Girl Mel C on Cliff Richard's Millennium Prayer.*

Where do you go after this? Do you get a Spice Girl?
— *Martyn Goff, Booker Prize administrator, on Jerry Hall's*

appointment as judge for the Whitbread
Prize.

I had a good time boxing. I enjoyed
it and I may come back
– Muhammad Ali.

It will be a triumph of confidence
over cynicism, boldness over blandness,
execellence over mediocrity
– Tony Blair on the Dome.

Men are a luxury, not a necessity
– Cher.

I empty the change out of his pockets
every night
– Christine Hamilton on her husband,
Neil.

In London there are school canteens
which refuse to take British beef
– Lionel Jospin justifies France's stand in
the beef war.

They are free people in a free country
– Spokesman for the Russian
Government on civilians in Grozny.

If we meet Germany again in the
future, do we get to keep them?
– Kevin Keegan, after being drawn
against Germany twice in a week.

2000

Week ending January 1, 2000

There's still no place on Earth that has our combination of qualities
— *Tony Blair on Britain.*

There are no votes in yesterday
— *John Major attacks William Hague.*

I hope he rots in hell
— *Sister Anne, a nun, of the man who raped her and left her for dead after a Christmas party.*

She forgets she is 99. She wears flimsy clothes and stands around chatting
— *Palace aide explains the Queen Mother's cold.*

Life is a more profound experience than we are told it is
— *The Prince of Wales in his Millennium message.*

A stunningly unoriginal idea
— *A critic of the Millennium poem by Andrew Motion, the Poet Laureate.*

The poetry world is very small and full of green-eyed snapping fish
— *Andrew Motion.*

We acknowledge that we have often fallen short of the example given us by the Prince of Peace in our treatment of others
— *Church leaders apologise for the wars, racism and sins committed in the name of Christianity.*

Humans are among the most naturally infertile animals
— *Lord Winston, a fertility expert.*

I'm no long-haired vegetarian rebel
— *Anti-foxhunting astronomer Patrick Moore.*

Week ending January 8, 2000

There have been mistakes
— *Lord Falconer on Dome delays.*

It was a very disappointing way to spend New Year's Eve
— *Greg Dyke, BBC director general, after failing to get to the Dome in time.*

The concept got blown out of all proportion
— *A firework designer defends the "River of Fire" along the Thames.*

The Queen was right
— *Burns expert explains that hands should not be held until the last verse of Auld Lang Syne.*

The most unwanted wanted man in the world
— *Lord Janner QC on the alleged war criminal Konrad Kalejs.*

I'd kill myself if I was that fat
— *Elizabeth Hurley ponders the charm of Marilyn Monroe.*

Were I to live for another 50 years there would be no job for me
— *Professor Gordon McVie, cancer specalist, foresees the disappearance of the disease.*

Blessed are the famous, for they will enjoy the praise of men
— *The Archbishop of Canterbury satirises modern values.*

The shadow of the gunman is being lifted
— *Millennium edition of the* Belfast Telegraph.

PR is dead in the water and it is not coming back
— *Labour MP Fraser Kemp on electoral reform.*

He likes to borrow my knickers
— *Victoria Beckham embarrasses her footballing husband.*

Week ending January 15, 2000

It would be difficult for a 45-year-old pregnant woman to leap over the barrier
— *Tony Blair's spokesman explains why Cherie paid for her train ticket and a fine.*

I have worked through three flu epidemics and this is not one
— *Dr Ian Bogle, chairman of the BMA.*

It would not have passed its MoT if it had been owned by anyone but the police
— *Broadcaster Sheena McDonald on the vehicle that knocked her down.*

I think a ban is rather silly
— *A black parent on a proposal to ban* Baa, Baa, Black Sheep *as racially offensive.*

I find him and his material quite offensive
— *Black comedian Curtis Walker on TV entertainer Ali G.*

I am enjoying that wonderful "I told you so" feeling
— *Stephen Bayley, who resigned after six months as creative director of the Dome.*

It was a bit of a laugh really, some of those toffee-nosed people having to queue
— *Frank Dobson, would-be Labour mayor of London on the Dome.*

He was crooked but OK
— *A prisoner vouches for Jonathan Aitken.*

I signed with as much excitement as when I first made love
— *Tycoon Ted Turner on the AOL/Time Warner merger.*

All I want to do is get back to my piano
— *Lord Lloyd Webber after buying the Stoll Moss theatre empire in London.*

Week ending January 22, 2000

There are a lot more young women on the electoral register than there are fight fans
– Lord Hattersley on allowing boxer and convicted rapist Mike Tyson into Britain

They are a bunch of frustrated women who want to be men
– Tyson on women's groups calling for him to be thrown out of the country.

Unlike President Clinton, I did inhale
– Mo Mowlam on cannabis.

It has obviously made a difference
– Jack Straw admits fall-out from the Stephen Lawrence inquiry has affected crime figures.

Bowls has a reputation as a boring game. I wanted to liven it up
– Tracy Seargeant after streaking at the at the Indoor Bowls Championship.

The destruction of the greatest police force ever
– Unionist councillor Jonathan Bell on reform of the RUC.

It is ridiculous that someone who reads the news gets paid ten times more than a nurse
– Kirsty Young, television newsreader.

There is a conspiracy of silence
– Lord Winston on the NHS.

It is about time I spread my wings
– Violinist Vanessa Mae who has sacked her mother as her manager.

Week ending January 29, 2000

Heaney has retrieved for the reading public a golden treasure
– Whitbread judge Dr Eric Anderson praises the winning poet's translation of Beowulf.

Republicans have been demonised for too long
– Gerry Adams speaks at an IRA funeral.

I'm still on cloud nine
– Jenson Button after becoming Britain's youngest Formula One driver.

An active and militant homosexual lobby is pushing for greater power
– Cardinal Thomas Winning.

He is not fit for the great office that he holds
– George Galloway on Cardinal Winning.

The proposal is based on a confusion between tolerance and moral judgment
– Chief Rabbi Dr Jonathan Sacks on changes to Section 28.

Being musical director of the Berlin Philharmonic is like being the Pope – except for the celibacy, I hope
– Sir Simon Rattle

Ties cause deafness in old age
– *James Dyson supporting the idea of casual dress for businessmen.*

It is good for me and for other women
– *Cancer patient Joanne Sprawson, 17, after the ban on using women's frozen eggs is lifted.*

The Prince said he was very proud of his ladies
– *Caroline Hamilton, leader of the all-female South Pole expedition after ringing the Prince of Wales.*

Week ending February 5, 2000

I have no doubt that each of your victims smiled and thanked you as she submitted to your deadly administrations
– *Mr Justice Forbes in his summing up at the trial of murderer Dr Harold Shipman*

Dr Shipman may have taken her life from us but he can never take our memories
– *The family of Jean Lilley.*

This was not a samurai sword. It was a chocolate eclair. I'm not a particularly brave person, but I'm not frightened of a chocolate eclair
– *Agriculture Minister Nick Brown after a female protestor attacked him with an eclair at a Farmers' Union conference.*

She should know that a fur hat is not just naff – it is a badge of shame
– *Mark Glover of Respect for Animals*

criticises Sophie Wessex for buying a fox-fur hat during her trip to St Moritz.

We have to consider how we would look now compared to the memories people have of us
– *Pop legends Abba explain why they turned down a £650 million offer to perform again.*

I think everyone needs a bit of breathing space
– *Peter Mandelson on the floundering peace process.*

I'll be Mr Mom
– *Michael Douglas promises to look after the baby while Catherine Zeta-Jones goes out to work.*

Now we're up and running, the wheel is as wonderful as we thought it would be
– *London Eye architect David Marks praises his creation.*

Week ending February 12, 2000

The fun and games down at the Assembly
– *Tony Blair on hearing of the resignation of the Welsh First Secretary whom he had just praised for doing an excellent job.*

They were cold, absent-minded and did not smile
– *Rossana Fuzzi, of Italian scooter manufacturer Aprilia, on the Spice Girls.*

There are a lot of similarities between our programmes

− Jörg Haider compares himself to Tony Blair.

In our love scene underwater, all I could think of was not drowning
− Virginie Ledoyen, co-star of The Beach *on why she did not succumb to Leonardo DiCaprio's charms.*

She wasn't interested in me. She's a very sophisticated European lady
− DiCaprio on Ledoyen.

Marriage is the right way to live. There is no moral equivalence between heterosexual and homosexual relationships
− Baroness Young defends Section 28.

If I thought it would fail I would never have come
− Pierre-Yves Gerbeau on his mission to save the Dome.

I have worked with more submarines than leading ladies.
− Sir John Mills, 91, on his career.

Nobody is asking for surrender by the IRA
− Peter Mandelson

The arms issue can be resolved
− Gerry Adams, leader of Sinn Fein.

Week ending February 19, 2000

If there was ever a case of dodgy goods falling on to the back of a lorry . . .
− Charles Kennedy on the Tory Save the Pound roadshow.

I phoned my wife only to be reminded that I had forgotten her birthday
− Alun Michael, after resigning as First Secretary of the Welsh Assembly.

You should be more modestly dressed in the house of the Lord
− A member of the Songs of Praise *congregation to scantily clad Eternal singer Easther Bennet.*

I have waited ten years to find out why I was left struggling for my life in the water
− Malcolm Williams on the inquiry into the Marchioness *riverboat disaster.*

At last the evil men have been named
− Social services whistle-blower Alison Taylor on a report on abuse in children's homes.

It is not a Muslim country. How could we stay? And the weather was depressing and the food was awful
− Freed Afghan hostage after arriving back in Afghanistan.

We're looking at names and all I can tell you is that it will be in keeping with the Somali-Bromley tradition
− David Bowie on hearing he is to be a father again at 53.

We must move quickly. History has taught us the danger of vacuums in Northern Ireland
− Bertie Ahern.

Week ending February 26, 2000

I don't think I have ever been patronised except by Jeffrey Archer, who called me "love"
— *Kirsty Wark.*

It's the most heinous crime not to declare the doughnut somebody gave you at lunch
— *Tory MP Teresa Gorman, alleged to have failed to declare interests.*

Just you try doing your VAT return with a head full of goblins
— *Terry Pratchett on whether he lives in his fantasy world.*

May I say how *relieved* I am to learn that all water has been passed by the Drinking Water Inspectorate
— *Letter to* The Times.

I trudge the streets rather than trade the soundbite. I am unspun
— *Frank Dobson, Labour candidate for mayor of London.*

We have become like an old married couple. We stand on platforms together and don't talk
— *Ken Livingstone on Frank Dobson.*

It's like putting Peter Rabbit in charge of the lettuce patch
— *Mother of Paddington train crash victim on Railtrack.*

I have never wanted to play for any other team since I was a boy

— *David Beckham after speculation may about a transfer.*

Week ending March 4, 2000

Far be it for me to admit that I don't know the answer
— *Tony Blair in Parliament.*

What a silly mistake I made
— *Jeffrey Archer reflects.*

I want to leave this cesspit in a coffin
— *Moors murderer Ian Brady argues for the right to die.*

Name another singer who's as good as me
— *Oasis frontman Liam Gallagher.*

I wanted to make him an honorary Rasta
— *Rita Marley on presenting the Prince of Wales with a tam hat with dreadlocks in Jamaica.*

You can't imagine the pleasure it gave me to sack her
— *Model agency boss John Casablanca on Naomi Campbell.*

You can no more be partly devolutionist than you can be partly pregnant
— *Charles Kennedy, Liberal Democrat leader.*

There are so many people with so little talent making so much money
— *Spice Girl Mel C.*

I proposed to Neil. It wasn't a question. It was an order
— *Christine Hamilton, wife of Neil.*

If those patients who had been classified as urgent had been operated on within a month we would probably have saved half of them
— *Peter Wilde of Bristol Royal Infirmary tells Tony Blair that a lack of cash is crippling his unit.*

The worst is far from over
— *Mozambique floods aid worker.*

Week ending March 11, 2000

Try to be as inconspicuous as possible when in public
— *Extract from the new security handbook for MPs.*

These people should be put on the first plane home
— *Lady Berry, who was pushed over by a Romanian woman begging in London.*

Mum's not very happy. She thought he'd be away for 12 months
— *Daugher of "castaway" ordered off Taransay by the BBC.*

Can we do that again? I made that crap
— *John Prescott, Deputy Prime Minister, after explaining his housebuilding plans on TV, unaware it was a live broadcast.*

We will do whatever it takes to protect the legitimate privacy of our family life

— *The Blairs on their former nanny's memoirs.*

This is proof that there is a God and he must be a Tory
— *Steven Norris, Tory candidate for London mayor, on Ken Livingstone's decision to stand as an independent.*

My problem is that I cannot be funny
— *Andrew Motion, the Poet Laureate.*

We want communication to be a two-way street with a lot of crossing between lanes
— *Pierre-Yves Gerbeau, Millennium Dome chief.*

So far as I was concerned it was just a crash, but the boss wanted more
— *Trevor Rees-Jones, Dodi Fayed's bodyguard in his book* The Bodyguard's Story.

Week ending March 18, 2000

You have to admire her. She hides her lack of talent so well
— *Manolo Blahnik, shoemaker, on Madonna.*

I'm not doing this to have a holiday in the Bahamas
— *Ken Livingstone on unregistered earnings of nearly £160,000 which he will use to fund his mayoral campaign.*

It's a bloody outrage. they could reduce the Midlands to an industrial wasteland
— *Trade union leader Sir Ken Jackson on BMW and Rover.*

An acutely embarrassing car
– *Jeremy Clarkson on the Rover 75.*

I have a good track record with larger-than-life iron ladies so I thought it would be a breeze
– *Carol Thatcher on researching the history of the QE2 for her new book.*

Every politician is allowed the occasional gaffe, if only to remind the public that they are still human
– *Peter Mandelson apologises for calling the Army's Household Division chinless wonders.*

I am much happier now I have joined the majority of people in this country who don't give a damn about politics
– *Christine Hamilton.*

If she chooses to live in Manhattan, she, like everybody else in this room, has to figure out how to pay the rent
– *Mick Jagger's lawyer contesting Luciana Morad's claim for more child support.*

Week ending March 25, 2000

I am not a mega or multi-millionaire, just an ordinary one
– *Delia Smith*

It feels like nothing, actually. I mean, it comes, it goes, right?
– *Michael Taylor, after falling share prices reduced his fortune by more than £6 billion in a day.*

My mum always told me to steer clear of redheads
– *Frank Dobson on red-haired Chris Evans's donation of £100,000 to Ken Livingstone's London mayor campaign.*

Frank Dobson's gaffes will pay for my entire campaign
– *Livingstone after Evans doubled his donation because of Dobson's remarks.*

Acting is just clowning around. Animal activism is something to make the world a better place
– *Actress Alicia Silverstone who runs an organisation for abused pets.*

It's time to bring back the bongs
– *Norman Baker MP calls for the reinstatement of News at Ten.*

A pissometer?
– *The Duke of Edinburgh in Australia when shown a piezometer, a device to measure water depth in soil.*

A modernised NHS, not private medical insurance, is the future
– *Tony Blair.*

The last time I saw anything like this was when McDonald's opened its first restaurant here
– *A policeman on the 15-mile eight-lane traffic jams when Ikea opened its first store in Moscow.*

Week ending April 1, 2000

The Bible is clear about witchcraft, demons, devils and the occult

– Primary school head on why she banned the Harry Potter books.

If we could get the common sense revolution to stand up and walk around it would look like Ann Widdecombe
– William Hague.

Maybe it would have been easier if I had been uglier
– Former Tory Minister Jonathan Aitken.

When I rang my bookmakers to obtain the odds on Saturday's University Boat Race I was asked the question: "Who is it between?"
– Letter to The Times.

I'd kill for cheekbones
– ITN newsreader Kirsty Young.

It's the biggest adrenaline rush I've ever experienced
– Sam Mendes on his Oscar for directing American Beauty.

You don't have cancer, it has you
– Ian Drury who died this week.

The people's poet laureate
– Madness frontman Suggs on Ian Drury.

It made me feel like crying
– Pete Goss after the break-up of his giant catamaran.

He's got a bit too much security and not enough ready cash
– A Big Issue *vendor kept waiting by*

the Prince of Wales while an aide found money.

I like the pews and I like the hymns and I like the orderliness of it all
– Novelist Fay Weldon after being baptised into the Chuch of England

Week ending April 8, 2000

What's your name?
– Sol Masters, three, on meeting the Queen at a school in Western Australia.

I don't like loud music
– Bill Wyman, Rolling Stone .

She laughs at all his awful jokes
– A friend of Prince Andrew's new love, Emma Gibbs.

He did the hand movements but not the dance routine
– Hotel owner on Prince William's karaoke version of the Village People's classic YMCA.

They take you to McDonald's, make you pay and ask if anyone is dating your sister
– Actress Minnie Driver on British men.

The institutions are hopping mad
– Banker after a computer crash brought the City to a standstill.

Microsoft placed an oppressive thumb on the scale of competitive fortune
– Judge Jackson rules against Bill Gates and Microsoft.

Popular uprising can sometimes work when appealing to the better nature of the banks might not
– *Junior Environment Minister Chris Mullin seems to be urging customers to boycott Barclays Bank over its closure of rural branches.*

A woman of my age is not supposed to be attractive or sexually appealing
– *Actress Kathleen Turner who appears naked as Mrs Robinson in a stage production of* The Graduate.

Week ending April 15, 2000

Just because I have made a point of never losing my accent it doesn't mean I'm an eel-and-pie yob
– *Michael Caine.*

Every year the international financial system kills more people than the Second World War. But at least Hitler was mad
– *Ken Livingstone.*

These results do not mean the Church is awash with cash
– *The Church of England, whose investments made £700 million last year.*

If the British soldiers on the beaches of Normandy in 1944 could look to the end of the century and see what England has become, they would not have bothered to advance up the beach
– *David Irving after his libel action defeat.*

His work is a tissue of lies, manipulation and distortion
– *Professor Deborah Lipstadt on David Irving.*

Yes, the Tories had a plan to save post offices – I'm sure King Herod had a plan to save the first-born as well
– *Charles Kennedy.*

This country is for blacks. But we need the knowledge of the whites to train people and create jobs
– *Zimbabwe's opposition leader, Morgan Tsvangirai.*

It's not cricket. Alas no. Not cricket but corruption
– *Christopher Martin-Jenkins after the South African cricketer Hansie Cronje admitted being "less than honest".*

Week ending April 22, 2000

What we reject is the persistence of vestigial attitudes of the Rhodesia of yesterday, of the master race, master colour, master employer
– *President Mugabe.*

If we beat Mugabe about the head, then he beats them about the head
– *Robin Cook on white Zimbabwean farmers.*

There have been times when I didn't think we would make 1,000, usually while standing outside a law court
– *Ian Hislop, editor of* Private Eye, *on its 1000th edition.*

He killed a man who invaded his home and is guilty of murder. But this should be a dire warning to all other burglars
– *Judge sentencing Norfolk farmer Tony Martin.*

It took two blonds to get me pregnant
– *Iman, wife of David Bowie, who borrowed fellow-model Christie Brinkley's baby for a day.*

We have seen European countries not able to support the Russian fight because they are afraid of a reaction among the Muslim inhabitants of Europe
– *Vladimir Putin on human rights in Chechnya.*

If you are going to come to Britain to seek asylum, you will first have to spend time in a camp
– *William Hague on asylum seekers.*

One cannot get bored by a bluebell
– *Sir David Attenborough.*

It was cheap in 1971 and it's even worse now
– *New York critic on staging of* Jesus Christ Superstar.

Week ending April 29, 2000

The products are worthless. The value is in the name. You can get any contract manufacturers to make them for you. They are two-a-penny
– *Richard Finn, former boss of Yardley, on cosmetics.*

He was good-looking in a sweet way and wasn't at all predatory
– *Mary Harron on Tony Blair, her boyfriend at Oxford.*

I enjoyed it out there. I love it. It's my second home
– *Andrew Halsey after trying to be the first disabled person to row solo across the Pacific.*

I know it's real. I was overwhelmed with negative feelings when touching it
– *David Bernstein on "Hitler's skull", on show in Moscow.*

He was totally right to shoot the men who broke into his home. I wish I'd been able to do the same
– *Mary Gill, 84, on farmer Tony Martin, after being left with a fractured skull by burglars.*

When a man's got to go, he's got to go
– *Michael Heseltine resigns.*

What this shows is the terrible criminal traffic in human misery
– *Jack Straw after witnessing the discovery of nine illegal immigrants at Dover.*

Cuba is the Ken Livingstone of the Caribbean, nourished by the overreaction of those who dread it
– *Libby Purves on the Elian affair.*

Is it possible to wear a beret back to front?
– *Letter to* The Times.

Week ending May 6, 2000

I love London. Compared to South America it is so . . . calm
– A Peruvian visitor, after the protest against capitalism.

It is only because of the bravery and courage of our war dead that these idiots can live in a free country at all
– Tony Blair after demonstrators defaced the Cenotaph and a statue of Churchill.

I don't speak French, I don't speak English, I am from Yorkshire
– Geoffrey Boycott.

Everyone is largely driven by their loins. Well, love can get you into trouble
– Graham Cluley, of anti- virus software company Sophos, on the ILOVEYOU virus that brought down computer systems everywhere.

We have had begonias three times their normal size and the lawn has never looked better
– Bristol gardener using fertiliser made from sewage by Wessex Water.

I don't know what I'm more disappointed about: the short cruise or not missing the London mayoral elections
– Passenger on the ill-fated cruise ship Aurora.

Dictators are people, too, you know
– Christopher Foyle, director of the
London bookshop, on regular customer Robert Mugabe.

It says something about our society when a third of the world has no food and we throw it around
– Ann Widdecombe, after being pelted with a custard pie.

Week ending May 13, 2000

It is a disgraceful state of affairs that we run a rail system that isn't safe
– Pam Warren, who has undergone 22 operations as a result of the Paddington rail crash.

We are living in an age of mass loquacity
– Martin Amis.

The incident was very, very minor
– Company boss Jim Hodkinson, sacked after touching a woman's bottom at a party.

I do feel like ringing Philip up and telling him to stop all this nonsense
– Major Ronald Ferguson on royal objections to Prince Andrew and Sarah remarrying.

I do not believe that the feeding of babies in either the chamber or committees is conducive to the efficient conduct of public life
– Betty Boothroyd.

I admit my show is the most stupid on TV
– Jerry Springer.

I feel prouder and more fulfilled than being awarded my PhD at Oxford
– *Ruth Lawrence, 28, who took a first-class degree from Oxford at 13, on becoming a mother.*

The jury is still out on this
– *Professor Gordon McVie of the Cancer Research Campaign on whether mobile phones are dangerous.*

It was a clear climate of slack
– *PCC chairman Lord Wakeham after criticising the share-dealing scandal at* The Mirror *newspaper.*

Week ending May 20, 2000

A simple air traffic control cock-up: they forgot the Airbus was waiting at the start of the runway
– *A pilot after two passenger jets came within 30 metres of colliding.*

It is the epitome of modern culture. You put this great heritage on your modern item and get it wrong
– *University lecturer Daniel Karlin on a Wordsworth sonnet incorrectly and prominently displayed at the London Eye.*

When nobody's calling me a broad, I prefer to be a Dame
– *Dame Elizabeth Taylor.*

Porn is really Viagra without damage to the liver
– *Fay Weldon.*

Nature has come to be regarded as a system that can be engineered for our own convenience
– *The Prince of Wales.*

We actually walked past the North Pole and went across to the Siberia side and then back-tracked
– *Corporal Alan Chambers on walking unaided to the North Pole.*

We had the happiest black faces in Africa in my time
– *Ian Smith, former rebel leader of Rhodesia, now Zimbabwe.*

Once she goes to sleep it takes a minor nuclear explosion to wake her
– *Tony Blair on Cherie.*

We have never seen anything like this in Copenhagen
– *The city's police chief after fighting between football fans.*

Week ending May 27, 2000

I had forgotten quite what an ordeal those last few hours of labour can be
– *Cherie Blair.*

He's gorgeous
– *Tony Blair on Leo.*

The Prime Minister has been working throughout the night on exhausting domestic matters
– *John Prescott, standing in at Prime Minister's Questions.*

I was very relieved when the child was born at the Chelsea and Westminster Hospital. I had thought he would be born in a manger
– Former Labour MP Leo Abse.

This is just like *Notting Hill*
– Hugh Grant on the media scrum outside the house that he shares with Liz Hurley.

I do not look forward to acting
– Bjork after winning Best Actress at the Cannes Film Festival.

John Gielgud to me was mercury – quicksilver in his wit, always ahead of the audience, always reassessing his performance
– Sir Peter Hall, theatre director.

With musical chairs the competition is not fair because it is always the biggest and strongest children who win
– Government warning on the dangers of the game.

The in-built amplifiers in the Lords benches create a lot of static. If you listen to debates for a long time your hair is left standing on end
– Lord Puttnam.

Week ending June 3, 2000

We have very little power beyond the ability to make noise
– Labour MP Austin Mitchell on the decline in MPs' influence.

Life is so short, it seems careless not to use it all
– Sir Trevor McDonald on why he is not retiring.

The gap between the ideal body shape and the reality is wider than ever
– British Medical Association on how models are thinner although women are getting heavier.

It is ironic that I get pilloried for alleged discrimination when my life's work has been devoted to widening access to education
– Professor John Stein on being criticised by Gordon Brown for rejecting Laura Spence's application to Oxford.

To us it is a normal car. We are not going to tell anyone who owned it
– Clive Sutton who is selling Tony Blair's former car for more than it originally cost.

It's a fairly unique position: to have been in charge of prison funding and then to have been an inmate. I wish I'd been more generous
– Jonathan Aitken.

If I'd known how much it meant to everybody, I'd have been too terrified to put my boots on
– Gary Lineker on how footballing success lifts the national mood.

Being thick isn't an affliction if you're a footballer, because your brains need to be in your feet ▾
– *Former manager Brian Clough.*

Week ending June 10, 2000

It would be strange if one of two of them did not think the Prime Minister was not the greatest living creature
– *A spokesman after the Prime Minister was jeered by a Women's Institute meeting.*

I saw people I would maim and kill. I felt nothing
– *David Copeland, alleged London nail bomber.*

I always get sentimental about £10,000
– *Steve Norris on being robbed of his Rolex.*

I'd hate to be really famous now. People seem to be only interested in who is doing what sexually to whom
– *Actress Julie Christie.*

If there is a next time I will take cold pizza
– *David Hempleman-Adams who ballooned over the North Pole.*

I don't want to be a caricature of myself
– *Singer Tom Jones asks women not to throw underwear at him during concerts.*

The introduction of exotic species like the grey squirrel into this country has done far more damage than a genetically modified potato
– *The Duke of Edinburgh on the GM debate.*

Has the world finally tired of worshipping at the shrine of small talents?
– *Richard Morrison in* The Times *on Madonna.*

This is the fifth day since my accident, the fifth day of my new life
– *Frankie Dettori after surviving a plane crash which killed the pilot.*

Week ending June 17, 2000

I am a very embarrassed man
– *Tony Fitzpatrick of the engineering company which constructed the "wobbly" Millennium Bridge.*

It feels like you have had a few drinks. We will come back when England have won and jump up and down and celebrate
– *Football fan's opinion of the bridge.*

It keeps people quiet, like religion used to
– *Actress Helen Mirren on football.*

To win we would have had to pay £47 million extra. We are spending public money. Could we really justify that?
– *Greg Dyke on the BBC's failure to acquire rights to Premiership football matches.*

Watching players who take their children on tour is the perfect contraception
– *Tim Henman.*

The Church is concerned with depth, not decor
– *The Bishop of London.*

I myself, my husband, children, neighbours and best friends would be imprisoned
– *Baroness Mallalieu on the consequences of a ban on hunting with hounds.*

This is anarchy and a perfect symbol of how law has broken down in this country
– *Local resident on travellers who could not be moved on from Hampton Court because it is royal property.*

I was lucky he was a thief and not keen on me
– *Julie Kirkbride MP on an armed intruder in her home.*

Week ending June 24, 2000

I am devastated, but to be honest we didn't play well enough
– *Kevin Keegan after England were knocked out of Euro 2000.*

Euro 2000 is a celebration of European football, not an excuse for a small minority of English fans to cause havoc
– *Uefa, after the England team were threatened with expulsion from the tournament.*

It was like an angel had been sent from heaven when the back door of the trailer was finally opened
– *One of only two survivors after 58*

illegal immigrants were found dead in the back of a lorry at Dover.

This is a profoundly evil trade whose perpetrators have no regard for human life
— *Jack Straw on the illegal trafficking of migrants.*

What is women's minister Tessa Jowell going to do — insist that Vanessa Feltz puts her weight back on?
— *Theresa May, shadow minister for women, on the Government's investigation into the media's influence on body image.*

Boyfriends have to understand me and my needs. They need to know what I want out of my life and about my strict regime
— *Tennis star Anna Kournikova.*

The farmyard noises they are making are not allowed in the House
— *Speaker Betty Boothroyd attempts to quieten Labour MPs during Prime Minister's questions.*

Week ending July 1, 2000

Without a doubt, this is the most important, most wondrous, map ever produced by mankind
— *Bill Clinton on the decoding of the human genome.*

I don't suggest that the Royal Family should close down and shut up shop, but if people want a monarch of the new century they should have a palace of the new century, in line with the architecture you see around London
— *Mo Mowlam urges the Royal Family to leave Buckingham Palace.*

The Queen lives in Buckingham Palace and I don't think she's intending to move and the Prime Minister doesn't think she should
— *A spokesman distances No. 10 from Mowlam's remarks.*

I am a realist. I do not believe it possible or desirable to prohibit newspapers entirely from speculation and reports about young ladies who might become a more permanent feature of his life
— *Lord Wakeham on media coverage of Prince William.*

It's more nerve-racking than cooking for Tony Blair
— *Jamie Oliver, who cooked his wedding breakfast.*

There was a time when those in public life attempted to behave with discretion and not like a stray mongrel in a public park
— *Lord Cobham, whose wife left him for former Conservative Cabinet Minister David Mellor.*

Week ending July 8, 2000

They are the rent boys of politics. The polite fiction that the Prime

Minister's advisers are responsible is absurd
– *Ken Follett attacking Tony Blair.*

What is so special about this family that they qualify for £7.9 million instead of 75p?
– *Dennis Skinner MP compares the Royal Civil List award and state pensions.*

Return to Scotland? I haven't gone yet
– *Sir Sean Connery, asked if he would return to live in Scotland.*

This is a joke. I hope you never get another day's sleep in your life
– *David Chell to Malaysian judge after a death sentence for drug trafficking charges which he denies.*

Even if we get her back it won't be the same Sufiah. If she is found she will need debriefing
– *Farooq Yusof, father of the child prodigy, claiming his daughter had been brainwashed.*

Let's concentrate on spin, not substance
– *Tony Blair makes a slip of the tongue during* Question Time.

I am so proud. If it was a script for a movie I wouldn't believe it
– *Richard Williams, father of Venus and Serena who met in the semi-final at Wimbledon.*

We are terrified. We stand on the street until 4am because we are too afraid to stay indoors

– *A Catholic mother after loyalists fired at her family as the marching season started in Belfast.*

Week ending July 15, 2000

Be happy for me
– *Betty Boothroyd to MPs after announcing her retirement as Speaker.*

You entered into the hearts of the British people and your own heart has been open to them ever since
– *The Archbishop of Canterbury on the Queen Mother.*

His faith was tinged with diffidence and, in a very Anglican way, forged by doubt
– *Terry Waite on Robert Runcie, the late Archbishop of Canterbury.*

You need bruises to know blessings and I have known both
– *Frances Shand Kydd after she almost drowned when she fell into a river while fishing..*

I didn't feel at my best this Wimbledon. I was out of sorts
– *Pete Sampras after winning his 13th Grand Slam title.*

I recently lost my security guards. There is nobody to collect the dry cleaning or go to the shops
– *Mo Mowlam, former Northern Ireland Secretary.*

Give the guy a break, give the guy a holiday

– Charles Kennedy, Liberal Democrat leader, on Tony Blair whom he described as "knackered".

My marriage is over, I'm single and I'm available. I can do what I like
– Liam Gallagher.

I will carry on writing, to be sure. But I don't know if I would want to publish again
– J. K. Rowling, author of the Harry Potter books.

Week ending July 22, 2000

The law is not a family-friendly profession
– Cherie Booth QC.

I have three policy announcements to underspin the strength of public finances
– Slip of the tongue by Chancellor Gordon Brown.

A blind school should beat Ecuador
– Former Davis cup captain David Lloyd before Ecuador beat England at tennis.

I'm not an outsider at all. I'm on every bloody A-list there is in the art world
– Artist Tracey Emin, of unmade bed fame.

I wouldn't let a bomb scare get in the way of something as special as this. I lived through the Liverpool Blitz
– Alma Brighouse at the 100th birthday pageant for the Queen Mother which was disrupted by bomb scares.

I hope you have enjoyed it as much as I have. It's been a wonderful evening
– The Queen Mother after her birthday celebrations.

It was lovely to talk to her, especially as I am a Windsor too
– Actress Barbara Windsor on receiving her MBE from the Queen.

I gave him drugs. He gave me Aids
– Liberal Democrat MP Dr Evan Harris on how he shared the health portfolio with a colleague.

Someone out there was watching us go through something no family should ever have to go through
– Sara Payne on the killer of her daughter Sarah.

Week ending July 29, 2000

I just keep saying to myself over and over again "I'm alive, I'm alive, I'm alive"
– Alice Brooking, who leapt from a first-floor room after Concorde crashed into her hotel.

It is a tragedy not just for them but for me also
– Richard Neale, a gynaecologist struck off for abusing his female patients.

If I was to say sorry I would be a hypocrite
– Loyalist killer Michael Stone on his release from prison.

You get rave reviews and sackfuls of fan mail. You must let me into the secret
— Tony Blair pays tribute to Betty Boothroyd as she retires.

This is the chief forum of the nation, today, tomorrow and I hope for ever
— Betty Boothroyd warns ministers against making important statements outside Parliament.

It's a lot easier to be famous than to be a decent person
— TV presenter Liza Tarbuck.

No one suggests that knowledge of racism makes you black. No one suggests that knowledge of anti-Semitism makes you Jewish. How can knowledge of homosexuality make you a homosexual?
— Lord Alli, a gay peer, on Section 28.

We have other attractions here that we are just as proud of
— County council leader on a proposal to boost tourism in Northamptonshire by calling it "Diana Country".

Week ending August 5, 2000

Show me the money
— American judge requires Mick Jagger to quantify his assets.

When therapy replaces faith and when therapeutic techniques are seen as the total answer to humanity's deepest needs and longings, another idolatry is introduced
— The Archbishop of Canterbury.

She never has a bet herself but, my goodness, she devours the *Racing Post*
— Sir Michael Oswald, the Queen Mother's racing manager.

Criticism of the peace process has become the closest thing to blasphemy
— Dame Jane Gow, whose husband was murdered by the IRA.

Two fried eggs in the gloaming
— A critic on what he saw when Jerry Hall removed her clothes for a scene in The Graduate.

I don't think fault is a useful idea
— BA boss Robert Ayling shrugs off any blame for the airline's problems after taking a pay-off close to £2 million.

When I started there was a nice atmosphere. The clients would come in for a chat and a cup of tea
— Josie Daly, who escaped conviction for running a multi-million-pound vice empire, reminisces on her early days as a brothel owner.

Less compassionate, more intolerant and just plain nasty
— Ian Massow on the Conservative Party after he defected to Labour.

Week ending August 12, 2000

Anyone who thinks I used to spend my holidays reading political tracts should have come with me for a week. There were barrels of wholesale John Smith's bitter and we used to have a pint at every stop
– *William Hague on his ability as a teenager to drink 14 pints a day while delivering the beer for his father's drinks business.*

Either we cancel that concession or the feed contains a contraceptive
– *Ken Livingstone, Mayor of London, on withdrawing the licence of the only official pigeon food seller in Trafalgar Square.*

Alec was very, very unusual. He was first of all, as you know, a very, very great actor but he was very, very retiring, shy, very charming and he had great humility
– *Sir John Mills, paying tribute to Sir Alec Guinness.*

It's not fair that the farmer has got all the money and he is the one that took Fred away
– *Mary Dolan, grandmother of the teenage burglar Fred Barras, on the family's decision to claim criminal injuries compensation after he was shot dead by farmer Tony Martin.*

God has given me more fame than any politician has
– *Imran Khan, the former Pakistan cricket captain and would-be Prime Minister of Pakistan.*

Week ending August 19, 2000

There is a clear smell of politics around this
– *A British Airways boss accuses the French of plotting to kill off Concorde by banning supersonic flights.*

Russian television is treating it like some sort of soap opera
– *Galina Belogun, wife of one of the crew of the stricken submarine* Kursk.

Don't make the mistake of thinking someone rules England. I just sit in and play the chief executive for a few weeks. It's better than working for a living
– *Deputy Prime Minister John Prescott describes his role while Tony Blair is on holiday.*

Belfast is like Islington, not Vietnam
– *Patrick Kielty, Northern Irish comedian.*

You would need someone more average looking
– *Heart-throb actor George Clooney turns down a role in a film of Nick Hornby's novel* About A Boy.

It is absurd to have an exam which everybody passes
– *Ruth Lea of the Institute of Directors on the rising A-level pass rate.*

Part of theatre is slightly to upset. It should elate, amuse and upset
– *Edinburgh Festival director Brian McMaster defends the staging of*

Barbaric Comedies, *which features graphic rape and copulation, after three-quarters of the audience walked out in disgust.*

Week ending August 26, 2000

I take a full sense of responsibility and blame for this tragedy. Words are not enough. I want to weep
– *Russian President Vladimir Putin on the* Kursk *disaster.*

Do you realise you are the first member of the Royal Family to win an Oscar?
– *US reporter interviewing Dame Judi Dench about playing Queen Elizabeth I.*

Politics is a younger and younger game. You don't get many elderly gents wandering around in the era of Tony Blair
– *Donald Dewar, Scotland's First Minister.*

I tend to favour covered arms, especially among violinists. You do not want to see too much flapping about
– *Leonard Slatkin, principal conductor of the BBC Symphony Orchestra.*

Let's go and face the music
– *Former spy David Shayler before his arrest on arrival at Dover.*

I live in fear of physical or verbal abuse
– *"Nasty" Nick Bateman, who was ejected from* Big Brother.

Australians are going to appear really ignorant
– *Professor George Kanarkis on the Olympic medals which depict Rome's Colosseum instead of the Parthenon in Athens.*

You can't get snow in temperatures like that, even if people thought it was. It was hail
– *Meteorological Office commenting on people sledging and snowballing in Hedon, East Yorkshire.*

Week ending September 2, 2000

My eventual aim is to be recognised first as a man and eventually as an author, poet and philosopher
– *Reggie Kray.*

All women should be able to look stylish. We've demonstrated that by using a real woman
– *The originators of the M&S advertisement using a size 16 model.*

I don't feel anything towards them
– *French fishermen's leader on British holidaymakers stranded by the protesters' blockade of ports.*

Making it "accessible" for a modern audience is a load of rubbish
– *Charles Dickens's great-grandson David on a film reworking of* A Christmas Carol.

Isn't *Big Brother* just *Teletubbies* without the costumes?
– *Letter to* The Times.

It is paternalistic and a terrifying restriction on Cupid
– *General John Gowans on a Salvation Army rule that officers may marry only other officers.*

It's a pity about the tree. It was pre-Armada
– *Lady Butler, 93, widow of "Rab" Butler, on an oak which fell at her home in Essex.*

I didn't actually find many facts, but I had a good time
– *Former sports minister Tony Banks on a recent fact-finding mission to Japan.*

I'm not being in a band with anyone who sounds like Elton John
– *Noel Gallagher of Oasis, criticising his brother Liam.*

Week ending September 9, 2000

Men always leave home to go to war, but women left home to go to peace
– *Jean Hutchison, peace campaigner, on leaving Greenham Common.*

Mo is loved by the people she comes into contact with and that is something political parties need more of, not less
– *Peter Kilfoyle, former Defence Minister, on Dr Mowlam.*

Truckers formed a club carrying her picture in their cabs as a pin-up
– *Mo Mowlam's husband, Jon Norton, after Lynda Lee Potter described his wife*

as *"an only slightly effeminate Geordie trucker".*

A wee, pretendy Parliament
– *Billy Connolly on Scotland's Parliament.*

Men are from *Maxim*, Women are from *Marie Claire*
– *Jane Gordon in* The Times *on the gender division between magazines.*

I have difficulty relating to it and I make no secret of that
– *David James, the latest saviour of the Millennium Dome.*

I've just got to get away after this match
– *Nasser Hussain after being out for a duck in both innings of a Test match.*

The communities which have not preserved the valid Episcopate . . . are not churches in the proper sense
– *Vatican declaration Dominus Jesus dismisses all Protestant churches as not the real thing.*

Week ending September 16, 2000

We will not give in to violence, to blockades or to threats. No one can seriously think that it is right for a British government to let policy be dictated by direct action of this sort
– *Tony Blair on the fuel blockade.*

I am not going to make decisions based on barricades and blockades, nor am I going to make decisions

based on the short-term volatility of the oil price
— *Gordon Brown.*

More people should try it. Our children are happier this way
— *Jerry Hall on being divorced from Mick Jagger.*

Never let me see you doing that again. Ours is a drinking party, not a reading party
— *A Tory grandee to the young Julian Critchley seen with his nose in a book.*

It's all about losing your brain without losing your mind
— *US actor Michael Fox on his fight against Parkinson's disease.*

But we'll starve
— *The Queen when it was suggested the Royal Warrant should be withdrawn from Harrods.*

There's no such thing as useless information
— *Magnus Magnusson, presenter of the TV quiz programme* Mastermind.

Week ending September 23, 2000

A week is a long time on the forecourt
— *Treasury spokesman on Labour's fuel-induced poll slump.*

I lied. I lied. My credibility will be in shreds. I lied. If this gets out, I'll be destroyed
— *Gordon Brown, according to a political*

exposé by Andrew Rawnsley, which claims the Chancellor lied in a radio interview.

You don't manhandle the monarchy
— unless you are a policeman
— *Buckingham Palace after the Princess Royal was touched on the arm by an official in Sydney.*

If I quit, it will be when we've launched an anti-ageing moisturiser, which is one of the biggest lies of the cosmetics industry
— *Anita Roddick, Body Shop boss.*

I do not believe it gives a green light for others to copy but it does show the law is with us
— *Lord Melchett, acquitted of criminal damage charges after Greenpeace campaigners destroyed a genetically modified crop.*

You never quite know what's going to happen next, but you try to give the impression that you do
— *Charles Kennedy admits what most other politicians dare not.*

I'm a little bit shocked at the moment . . . something strange happened
— *Cyclist Jason Queally from Chorley, Lancashire, after winning a gold medal in the men's 1-km time trial and setting a new Olympic record.*

Week ending September 30, 2000

I am not some prim Brownie pack leader; in fact, I am a bit of a bitch
— *Delia Smith.*

Everything makes sense on 14 pints.
Michael Portillo looks loyal. And
even William Hague looks like a
Prime Minister
– *Tony Blair.*

I couldn't even walk properly but
this is the Olympics, so you call on
everything in your body and soul
– *Denise Lewis who won gold in the
heptathlon despite injury.*

You can't live in America and not be
shocked by ignorance. People living
in Florida have no idea where
Florida is, and that's the easy one
because it sticks out
– *Historian Simon Schama on a survey
suggesting many youngsters thought the
Battle of Britain was in 1066.*

The widespread and undetected use
of drugs makes the whole thing
pointless
– *Comedian Alexei Sayle on the
Olympics.*

When you are looking down the
barrel of a gun, the last thing you
need is a ball-point pen
– *Andy McNab, former SAS undercover
operator, now a novelist, on whether the
pen is mightier than the sword.*

Week ending October 7, 2000

I have no intention of uttering my
last words on the stage, darling.
Room service and a couple of
depraved young women will do me
quite nicely for an exit
– *Actor Peter O'Toole.*

It's better for my daughter to be
brought up in a single-parent family
than in an unhappy marriage
– *J. K. Rowling after donating £500,000
to the National Council for One Parent
Families.*

The three-piece suit will die off
because there is a generation which
thinks suits represent an authority it
doesn't trust
– *Martin Raymond, senior lecturer at the
London School of Fashion.*

Safety has to be the prime suspect of
our service
– *Announcer apologising for the delay in
a London-Leeds train because of a bomb
scare.*

If you want to be happy for a short
time, get drunk; happy for a long
time, fall in love; happy for ever, take
up gardening
– *Arthur Smith, the comedian and
playwright.*

I'm 5ft 4³/₄ tall, so I have to stand on
a box or I'd never reach the Hebrides
– *Helen Young, BBC weather forecaster.*

You play into the hands of criminals
if you make the law into an ass
– *Lord Cranborne on Ann Widdecombe's
proposal for zero tolerance on cannabis
possession.*

Week ending October 14, 2000

A successful man is a man who makes more money than his wife can spend. And a successful woman is a woman who can find such a man
— *Bienvenida Buck.*

That's purity, 'cos Reg leaves the Earth a gent. All pure
— *A mourner at Reggie Kray's funeral on why he was wearing a white armband.*

This is Trafalgar Square, not Red Square
— *People for the Ethical Treatment of Animals (Peta) on Ken Livingstone's campaign to rid the square of pigeons.*

I was walking across King's Cross station when a drunken Irishman flung his arms around me. He wanted to thank me for the peace process in Northern Ireland
— *Ann Widdecombe on being mistaken for Mo Mowlam.*

Where has the role of parents gone? Why aren't they telling their children where acorns come from and how to tell a chicken from a pheasant?
— *Teachers' union leader David Hart commenting on a survey by* Country Life *revealing children's ignorance of rural matters.*

In a world often of intrigue he was a man of integrity, in a world of ambition he was a man of service
— *The Prime Minister on the late Donald Dewar.*

If you vote for us next year she will show you both of them
— *Richard Madeley, husband and co-presenter of* This Morning, *after his wife Judy Finnegan's jacket fell open to reveal her bra at the National Television Awards.*

Whiteness nowhere features as an explicit condition of being British, but it is widely understood that Englishness, and therefore by extension, Britishness, is racially coded
— *From a report,* The Future of Multi-Ethnic Britain.

Week ending October 21, 2000

One was big and one was tiny. I scared them away with my stick
— *Cameron Munro, three, describing the dinosaurs he encountered on his night alone in the woods.*

I haven't a clue why they sent it to me. As far as I know I haven't got a reputation as a receiver of stolen goods
— *Jeremy Paxman on being sent the stolen Enigma coding machine.*

The number of broken rails fell last year to 917 but that is far too high. You wouldn't want that many planes having broken wings
— *Spokesman for the Rail Regulator.*

Are we really to treat the heir to the throne as something no better than a laboratory rat?

– *Author Michael Dobbs on Lady Gavron's view that the Prince of Wales should have married a black woman.*

It would not be tolerated in any other workplace. It would be called institutional bullying and people would be off to consult the union
– *Tessa Kingham, Labour MP, on life in the House of Commons.*

Moisturisers do work. The rest is pap. There is nothing on God's earth that will take away 30 years of arguing with your husband
– *Anita Roddick, founder of the Body Shop.*

Being a mother means you never want to take your clothes off on television again
– *Actress Imogen Stubbs.*

He didn't like heads, did he?
– *John Prescott, Deputy Prime Minister, opening an exhibition of Henry Moore's sculpture in Beijing.*

It makes you a better survivor because you have to be on the alert. You can't go home
– *Viscount Linley on the virtues of boarding school.*

When she was nice she was very, very nice. Some of the time she was horrid
– *Patrick Jephson, former aide to Diana, Princess of Wales, defending his book about her.*

I rather regret admitting having used cannabis, considering what bad company I seem to be keeping
– *Mo Mowlam.*

Week ending October 28, 2000

It's different from the old tenement room I was brought up in
– *Michael Martin, the new Speaker of the House of Commons, on his Palace of Westminster residence.*

I've never seen so much female vanity. Some of them spend two-and-a-half hours in make-up. It's like a locker room in here
– *Shirley MacLaine on Liz Taylor, Debbie Reynolds and Joan Collins, her co-stars in a new film.*

I have never seen a nightingale in Berkeley Square
– *Dame Vera Lynn, famed for her singing of "A Nightingale Sang in Berkeley Square".*

There is even a rose named after me. The catalogue describes it as "superb for bedding"
– *June Whitfield, the actress.*

I do not mind what language an opera is sung in so long as it is a language I don't understand
– *Sir Edward Appleton, eminent physicist.*

We could go for marriage, an affair or casual sex
– *Paddy Ashdown to Tony Blair about*

Liberal co-operation with the Labour Party.

There is no doubting my philosophy and what will remain with me for as long as the blood runs through my veins: the red blood of socialism
– Betty Boothroyd, the former Speaker.

The state of their leaves shows if they are unhappy
– Spokesman for the Royal Botanic Gardens, Edinburgh, on the fig trees in Westminster's new Portcullis House, which are shedding their leaves.

My life is like a B-movie. There were police and guns everywhere
– Barbara Windsor on being caught in a siege at a Chinese restaurant.

I remember thinking the first time I had a baby: now here is a sport that I can do
– Sheila Kitzinger, the guru of natural childbirth.

If I am wary of sentimental pieties about the theatre it's because I often find it moribund, irrelevant, sclerotic, old-fashioned and dull
– Sir Richard Eyre, the director.

At Oxford we drank to ludicrous excess and threw up over some of the most beautiful buildings in Britain
– Steve Norris, unsuccessful Tory candidate for Mayor of London.

Week ending November 4, 2000

If you don't get a rich husband, I cannot see the point of a husband
– Ruby Wax.

We may not have a government machine, but we have got the British people. It's David and Goliath, but David has more stones
– Mark Francis, fuel protester.

We are already dealing with floods which are probably the most widespread since 1947 and in some places as severe. The misery is set to continue
– Sir John Harman, chairman of the Environment Agency.

It was wild. It makes me quite nervous to go outside
– Patrick Moore on the tornado that struck his home town of Selsey, West Sussex, the second to hit the town.

Dad, don't believe everything you read. You're not nearly as cool as the people think you are
– George W. Bush's twin daughters.

The bedtime story is a marker for other values and beliefs in the family and in society at large
– Dr Aric Sigman, psychologist, after finding that more than half of British parents say they don't have time to read their children to sleep.

I assume the event wasn't organised by the council's press department
— *Tony Banks, Labour MP, after being robbed at knife point on the day when a local anti-violence campaign began.*

The present Government are a load of philistines. And that's not surprising. What is surprising is that they are a lot more philistine than the last lot
— *Artist David Hockney.*

To have one's back described as scrawny is heavenly — I can go and eat cream buns for a week
— *Author Jilly Cooper's riposte to the late Woodrow Wyatt's description of her.*

I have become an accidental celebrity. And, truly, it wasn't hard to do
— *Monica Lewinsky.*

He is not leaving under a cloud
— *Spokesman for the Met Office commenting on the resignation of John Kettley, the BBC weatherman.*

Billy is an ideal present for the Queen. He would easily fit in with the mounted deer heads and stuffed animals at Balmoral
— *Malcolm Ford, importer of the cult fish novelty Big Mouth Billy Bass.*

Week ending November 11, 2000

It's not in any way clear that I have lost, and until it is clear I can't concede
— *Al Gore to George W. Bush after the*

pivotal Florida vote in the American presidential campaign proved too close to call.

We haven't been up this late in years
— *Barbara Bush, mother of George W.*

The people have spoken, but it's going to take a while to determine what they said
—*President Bill Clinton after the presidential election failed to produce a clear result.*

It was like something out of a James Bond movie
— *Millennium Dome trapeze artist after police foiled an attempt to steal £350 million worth of De Beers diamonds from the controversial attraction.*

Edith Nesbit was a great writer, but she was not a terribly sensible mother
— *Jenny Agutter, star of* The Railway Children, *after Railtrack said that the film had caused real-life accidents.*

The secret is to smile and mouth the word "sex"
— *Sir Norman Wisdom, 85, on how to appear at your best in front of the cameras at a photocall.*

It has always been my aim to live a life so openly scandalous that I would be immune from blackmail
— *Lord Beaumont of Whitley, the Green Party peer.*

To be a good campaigner, you have to be prepared to be a bore and to be

labelled a bore. I have never flinched from boring people
– *Tam Dalyell, Labour MP.*

The present severe weather conditions in our country are, I have no doubt, the consequences of mankind's arrogant disregard of the delicate balance of nature
– *The Prince of Wales.*

I needed to be able to sit there for six to seven hours and I think I did that well
– *Vladimir Kramnik, the new World Chess Champion, on defeating Garry Kasparov, his former mentor.*

I know I have madness in me somewhere, but I recognise that and accept it
– *Patrick Marber, playwright and theatre director.*

Week ending November 18, 2000

I don't have anybody to leave money to. I am a single man. I like to spend money
– *Elton John on spending £40 million in 20 months.*

I felt my chest deflate, blood enter my mouth and air exhale through the wound. I believed I had been fatally stabbed
– *George Harrison, the former Beatle, in a written statement during the trial of the man who attacked him and his wife Olivia. Harrison shouted "Hare Krishna" at his assailant.*

To cut ourselves off from the major strategic alliance on our doorstep would be a supreme act of folly
– *Tony Blair on why we should be politically involved in Europe.*

The choice is whether the voters are going to win this election by having every vote count
– *Al Gore, the American presidential candidate, demanding a full recount in Florida.*

They all said you wouldn't come or that you would only come in small numbers, but they want to take a good look around here today and take a look down the motorway
– *David Handley, the fuel protester, addressing demonstrating truck drivers in Hyde Park, London.*

They seem to have lost the vigour of breeding in the past two years because they are getting too inbred
– *Graham Stone, "Keeper of the Royal Budgerigars", on the birds' problem.*

We need to get away from rail steam heritage. Why should aviation have a much more intellectual approach to safety management than the railways?
– *Sir Alistair Morton, chairman of the Strategic Rail Authority.*

I was named after my father and I was knighted in his name because I love my father
– *Michael Caine, the actor, after being knighted Sir Maurice Micklewhite.*

No sooner had I invited her to join me on the dance floor than the Marine Band broke into a spirited rendition of "The Lady is a Tramp". Only narrowly did we avert an international incident, not to mention a court martial or two
— *Gerald Ford, the former American president, recalling a White House incident involving the Queen.*

You cannot encounter a Rubens 10ft by 15ft on a laptop
— *Maggie Hambling, the painter and sculptor, on people who call up the National Gallery on the web.*

Ask for an upgrade
— *Ivana Trump, when questioned about how to overcome the discomforts of economy class air travel.*

I asked, "Master, would it be all right to wear a fringe when I'm on stage?" He said: "What a very good idea. It would hide that hideous expanse of forehead"
— *Actress June Whitfield, recalling what Noël Coward told her.*

Week ending November 25, 2000

The coverage has made me out as "posh dosh". And it is all so incredibly inaccurate
— *Judith Keppel, cousin of Camilla Parker Bowles, who won £1 million on* Who Wants to be a Millionaire?

Railways are not a top priority
— *Tony Blair's opinion in 1997, as revealed in leaked Cabinet papers.*

Well, they are now
— *Libby Purves in* The Times.

I do have to pinch myself to make sure I'm not dead
— *Film actress Lauren Bacall, 76.*

What seemed to drive her with particular force is the pursuit and retention of money
— *Ian Mill QC referring to Maria Church, mother of singer Charlotte, who was sued by Jonathan Shalit, her daughter's ex-manager.*

This sandbag means a lot to people in my country
— *John Prescott, who took a sandbag to the podium for his speech to the Climate Conference in The Hague.*

In view of the spending habits of Sir Elton John, could he be persuaded to move around the country a bit to even up the North–South divide
— *Letter to* The Times.

To say that change at Westminster happens at a snail's pace is to insult the pace of snails
— *Labour MP Oona King.*

They have let me and their country down
— *Clive Woodward, manager of the England rugby team which threatened to go on strike.*

We're trying to get away from the old WH Smug image to be more flexible and modern
— *Beverley Hodson, managing director of WH Smith, on plans to reintroduce porn magazines to the shops.*

I don't like shaking hands with people because, you know, where do they come from?
— *Donald Trump.*

I don't think the feminist movement has done very well for itself. They made blunder after blunder after blunder. I hope next time there's an upsurge in feminism they'll do a little better
— *Doris Lessing.*

I've learnt to be more relaxed and less obsessive, less selfish — but that's being a parent
— *Madonna.*

Thank God I am an actress, because otherwise I would have placed all of that energy on one after another of you and made you insane
— *Meryl Streep to her children.*

I also think of dressing as a way of being artistic, and art is something I'm quite into
— *England footballer David Beckham.*

There are too many thickos in English football
— *Francis Maude, Shadow Foreign Secretary.*

Week ending December 2, 2000

The prejudice that beauty and brains are incompatible is fading. Do you have to be dumb if you are beautiful?
— *Priyanka Chopra, Miss India.*

Macho invetere
— *Dominique Voynet, the French environment minister, on John Prescott.*

I'm accused of being macho man. Moi?
— *John Prescott's response.*

He had a good life in Nigeria with everything. He wanted to be a doctor
— *Richard Taylor, father of ten-year-old Damilola, who was stabbed to death on a South London estate.*

I became a barrister because I hated my father; my father hated lawyers
— *Clarissa Dickson Wright, surviving one of Two Fat Ladies.*

This train will call at Garforth, East Garforth, Micklefield and Ulleskelf, due to arrive in York, whenever
— *Announcement on a Manchester to York train.*

My mother was worried about whether my father would be wearing pyjamas or a mackintosh in the afterlife
— *Jazz singer George Melly.*

The cross I had to bear
— *The Rev Carol Stone, formerly Rev Peter Stone, after a sex change.*

Reading Harry Potter books out loud is more fun than I feel a single human being could ever deserve. It is like swimming in chocolate
– *Stephen Fry, whose eight-hour recording of* Harry Potter and The Philosopher's Stone *was broadcast on Radio 4.*

The fact that everyone assumes sex scenes to be autobiographical is an aspect of being married to a novelist that my husband has borne with enormous fortitude
– *Wendy Holden, a nominee for the Bad Sex in Fiction Award.*

I'd be a complete mess if I had
– *Charles Aznavour, the French singer, when asked if he had lived the torments of his songs.*

All the bad publicity does toughen you up. The only way you can deal with the criticism is by learning not to care
– *Simon Le Bon of Duran Duran.*

I personally look forward to the day when we have a British football team. I think we might start winning some games
– *Jack Straw, Home Secretary.*

You really have to be tanned and fully waxed. You couldn't wear this with a lot of chest hairs poking through. That would be horrible
– *David Furnish, Elton John's partner, describing one of the singer's lacy shirts.*

I have no ambition to be leader of the Conservative Party
– *Michael Portillo.*

I would say: "I'm going to call you Andrew. You call me Peter." To which they would then say, "Yes, Minister"
– *Peter Hain's experience of protocol at the Foreign Office.*

Week ending December 9, 2000

I can't make peace with it because I know I'm going to die from it. There's always a feeling: "Why did it hit me?"
–*Dudley Moore talking about progressive supranuclear palsy.*

It seems to me the mark of a civilised society that certain privileges should be taken for granted such as education, health care and the safety to walk the streets.
– *Alan Bennett.*

He wanted to improve himself. He came out of a library, not an amusement arcade
– *Richard Taylor on the last moments of his murdered son Damilola.*

I'm no gold-digger. I'm self-sufficient . . . Pre-nups are brilliant
– *Catherine Zeta-Jones on her marriage to Michael Douglas.*

It will be a good idea to hit targets on the English mainland again . . . At times it's a necessary evil for civilians to be killed
– *Dorothy Robinson, head fundraiser of*

Cla na Gael, a clandestine Irish-American organisation that has raised hundreds of thousands of pounds for the IRA.

We should do something that will make your heart dance once a day. If you can't do that because you're too depressed, then do something that will make somebody else's heart dance
– Yoko Ono.

The archbishop is not just another international business executive. He is a priest and spiritual leader who must have time for reflection, reading and prayer as well as the nurture of unhurried human contact
– A report calling for a third archbishop to be appointed in the Church of England.

I do not watch drama because it depicts cohabitation, promiscuity, infidelity, adultery and under-age sexual activity as not just normal but as mature and desirable. You may wonder how I know it does that without watching it: the Bishop of Winchester says so
– Edward Enfield, father of comedian Harry Enfield.

She had arrived after a prodigious amount of the prancing about in fancy dress which the British call History
– Matthew Parris on the Queen's arrival at Parliament.

A multi-agency project catering for holistic diversionary provision to young people for positive action
– Luton Education Authority's description of go-karting lessons.

The First Minister is responsible for many things, but Madonna is not one of them
– David Steel, Presiding Officer of the Scottish Parliament, when asked about the pop diva's plans to get married in Scotland.

Everybody should practise flirting because it's an art form
– Advice on how to behave at an office party from Heather Pickering, whose firm offers courses in good manners, social skills and etiquette.

Week ending December 16, 2000

I wish people would realise I'm serious
– Claudia Schiffer on her plans to be an actress.

It's absolute hell travelling on the railways at the present time
– Tony Blair.

Peace is not a spectator sport . . . The enemies of peace don't need your approval. All they need is your apathy
– President Clinton speaking in Northern Ireland.

Fun-loving guy seeks peace
– Sinn Fein's Gerry Adams when asked what his lonely hearts advertisement might read.

I am depressed. Not foaming at the mouth. Not in a moral frenzy. Not wailing for a lost age of chastity. Just depressed
– Times *columnist Libby Purves on the news that the morning-after pill is to be available over the counter.*

If there's a toss-up between being a long-term malingerer to screw an extra sixpence out of the police or getting on with life, I'd rather get on with life
– *TV presenter Sheena MacDonald who sustained severe head injuries after being knocked down by a police van answering a 999 call.*

We feel that no matter what we do we are going to upset somebody. Morale is at rock bottom
– *A London police officer.*

Although we may never know with complete certainty the identity of the winner of this year's presidential election, the identity of the loser is perfectly clear. It is the nation's confidence in the judge as an impartial guardian of the rule of law
– *Justice John Paul Stevens, dissenting American Supreme Court judge.*

We cannot do business like this in the future
– *Tony Blair after two hours' sleep at the Nice summit where, after five days' wrangling, final agreement on a treaty fell below the hopes of many European Union countries.*

We mustn't get carried away but let's say for once: "Brilliant, well done"
– *England cricket captain Nasser Hussain after the victory over Pakistan.*

The passionate political rutting and twittering at Westminster are definitive evidence of an impending election
– *TV presenter Gavin Esler.*

It feels like Beatlemania is back
– *Sir Paul McCartney on news that the Beatles compilation album has topped UK charts for a month and sold 12 million copies worldwide.*

The Pope rang me while I was watching *Dynasty*
– *Bob Geldof.*

I wanted to see the world and help people
– *Prince William on why he went to Chile on the Raleigh International expedition.*

Put a point and I'll give you a straight answer
– *Mohammed Al Fayed addressing Anthony Boswood, Neil Hamilton's QC, in the Court of Appeal.*

The last time a babe in arms appeared on a Downing Street Christmas card, it was Jesus. This year it is Leo Blair
– The Times *on the Blairs' card.*

Week ending December 23, 2000

She may be the Queen of Pop, but she's not the Queen Mum
– *Scottish police on why Madonna did not get a motorcycle escort upon arriving in Inverness.*

We conclude that the Queen no longer speaks in the Queen's English of the 1950s
– *Professor Jonathan Harrington, of Sydney's Macquarie University, after studying the Queen's vowels.*

Taking part in battle is not like going to the office
– *General Sir Charles Guthrie on the proposed recruitment of disabled people to the armed forces.*

We thought there was going to be an empty chair at the table for Christmas
– *Anne Winder, twice told her son Paul was dead after he was held hostage in Colombia by guerrillas, who finally released him and his companion Thomas Hart Dyke.*

It is a dangerous sport; the boxers know that when they get into the ring
– *Promoter Frank Warren after the bout that left boxer Paul Ingle fighting for his life.*

Tizzy, I accidentally rang your mobile phone yesterday and your voice answered
– *The father of Elizabeth Gold, 17, who*

died in an apparent suicide pact with a friend, speaking at her memorial service.

It will be a very traditional Christmas, with presents, crackers, doors slamming and people bursting into tears, but without the big dead thing in the middle. We're vegetarians
– *Victoria Wood.*

This is really the bottom end of the counterfeit market
– *David Westcott of Essex County Council on the discovery of thousands of pairs of fake underpants.*

Camelot has been given a licence for life to print money
– *Sir Richard Branson after the failure of his bid to run the National Lottery.*

If I'm buying clothes I'll go to Top Shop, but if someone else is paying I prefer DKNY
– *Charlotte Church, the singer.*

Clinton is, I can assure you, more sausage than sizzle
– *Peter Mandelson.*

It was the coldest I have ever been or ever want to be. Swimming in December is not a good idea
– *Richard Jones after rescuing a family whose car had fallen into a river.*

Women want men to change, but they don't. Men want women to stay the same, but they can't
– *Shirley Conran.*

I wouldn't have wanted to be a politician. It would worry me too much, supporting decisions I didn't believe in. It's hard enough supporting the Church of England sometimes
— *Dr Robert Hardy, Bishop of Lincoln.*

It's like something out of a film. I can't even drive
— *Singer Billie Piper on the Ferrari brought for her by DJ Chris Evans.*

When impertinent reporters ask if I'm gay, I say, "I'm mildly cheerful" ▼
— *Sir Arthur C. Clarke.*

Week ending December 30, 2000

What a ridiculous thing to do
— *The Princess Royal, snapping at a wellwisher who offered her a floral basket.*

We are not a fuddy-duddy organisation wanting to ban nipples
— *Christopher Graham, director-general of the Advertising Standards Authority.*

Is it a criminal offence to chop some holly off a neighbour's tree for our Christmas decorations?
— *999 caller to Staffordshire Police.*

The main aim of education should be to send children out into the world with a reasonably sized anthology in their heads so that, while seated on the lavatory, waiting in doctors' surgeries, on stationary trains or watching interviews with politicians, they may have something interesting to think about
— *John Mortimer.*

I'd sooner go to Vladivostock
— *Terry Wogan, when offered free tickets for the Millennium Dome.*

The year that felt like 40 years
— *Pierre-Yves Gerbeau on his period as boss of the Millennium Dome.*

I only went to the company for a fortnight under the school's work placement scheme
– Adam Hughes, a 17-year-old schoolboy who saved a printing firm from bankruptcy by introducing new sales techniques.

That's what City men are like – full of bullshit one minute, then sending you flowers or shedding a little tear if you tell them a sob story the next
– Tricia Jamal, remembering life as Britain's first woman City trader.

The family of the 21st century is facing some very serious challenges
– The Archbishop of Canterbury.

To say it was a living hell is an understatement. The conditions were utterly barbaric and every day seemed like a month
– Ian Bamling, a teacher released from a United Arab Emirates jail after two years' imprisonment for possessing a tiny amount of cannabis, which he has always denied.

Did the jury realise they were giving me a life sentence of humiliation and penury? Perhaps it was all a game to them
– Extract from the newly published diary of former Tory MP Neil Hamilton after his failed libel action against Mohammed Al Fayed.

I'm not modest. If I was lousy I say I was lousy. But if I'm good, can't I say I'm good?
– Kirk Douglas on his acting career.

She has had a remarkable life with me with remarkable privileges
– Lord Archer on his wife Mary.

I got lucky . . . I wasn't handsome. I had a baby face. But I was pretty – so pretty that actresses didn't want to work with me
– Roger Moore on his early acting success.

People get angry at Mike Tyson for saying he's going to rip his opponent's heart out. What do they think warriors do at night – read Tennyson?
– Billy Connolly.

2001

High faces of pure white, harshly disfigured by deep blue cracks roughly cut from above
— *Ellen MacArthur, round-the-world sailor, on the icebergs she is passing in the Southern Ocean.*

Hamlyn is not a sleazy figure, but the way the party was acting you would have thought it had taken money off a serial killer
— *A Labour MP on Lord Hamlyn's £2 million donation to Labour.*

Our energy-burning lifestyles are pushing our planet to the point of no return
— *The Archbishop of Canterbury.*

Nothing would be sadder than to have the place shut down for six months while we try to decide what to do with it
— *Simon Jenkins, Millennium Commissioner, on the Dome.*

He was the first [barrister] who understood it was all about playing to the jury rather than convincing the judge
— *Ian Hislop, editor of* Private Eye, *on George Carman QC.*

One of my objections to religion is that it prevents the search for God
— *Sir Arthur C. Clarke.*

There are 183 performance criteria but it does not mention the word "bus" once
— *Guy Gibson on the bus driver's manual he has translated into plain English.*

This was supposed to be the issue to unite mankind for the new century, but that was when leaders could be seen with Diana
— *Ken Rutherford, of the Landmines Survivors Network, on the decrease in support for landmine clearance since the death of Diana, Princess of Wales.*

If only I'd known never to trust a lawyer. One should only turn to a lawyer as a last resort, because they exploit the worst in people
— *Martin Bell, independent MP.*

The National Trust can be seen as an organisation that's middle class and slightly remote
— *Fiona Reynolds, new director-general of the National Trust.*

Someone who is to be remembered for dressing well does not remove her clothes in public
— *Eleanor Lambert, 96, American doyenne of fashion and compiler of a best-dressed list, chiding Nicole Kidman for appearing nude in a play,* The Blue Room.

I have friends who are waiters who go foxhunting and I have friends who are dukes who don't
– *Derek Laud, an advocate of foxhunting who describes himself as the "first Afro-Saxon".*

They are just another crop, like cotton was in the past
– *Lord Glenconner, who lives in the Caribbean, on tourists.*

Mathematicians have no friends except other mathematicians, are not married or seeing anyone, usually fat, unstylish, wrinkles in their forehead from thinking so hard, 30 years old, a very short temper
– *Schoolchild's description of a typical maths teacher.*

Week ending January 13, 2001

What annoys me most is that the more terribly thin and fit actresses we have the less real our films become
– *Kate Winslet.*

The BBC is hideously white
– *Greg Dyke, BBC director-general.*

She should have a health warning tattooed on her forehead
– *Sir Roy Strong on artist Tracey Emin.*

It is good for the people to see the King and Queen having a hamburger at Planet Hollywood
– *King Abdullah of Jordan.*

I could have decided not to mention racism at all and stuck to policing questions. But as this progression of coppers came in, our mouths sort of fell open and we thought: "We are bloody well going to have the courage to say it all publicly"
– *Former High Court judge Sir William Macpherson defending his report on the Stephen Lawrence case.*

Being naked is not a sin
– *Artist Vincent Bethell after being cleared in court of causing a public nuisance by being naked.*

It is frighteningly simple to knock up in your kitchen
– *Dr Winstock of the National Addiction Centre on a new drug sweeping the nation.*

To talk of me as Mr Big is ridiculous. I couldn't organise my way out of a paper bag
– *"Costa crook" Clifford Saxe who has been on the run since 1984.*

It felt like an enforced six-hour stop-over at a second-rate German airport
– *Martin Amis on visiting the Millennium Dome.*

Melvyn Bragg is to the arts what those parasitic birds are to a rhino. Irritating, but ultimately not significant
– *Sir John Drummond, former controller of Radio 3.*

People think Islington is all canapés with Tony and Cherie. But we have council estates the size of the Gobi Desert
– *Tony Parsons, author and broadcaster.*

I've slept on floors all over the world, with a multitude of different people, but we didn't have sex
– *Vanessa Redgrave on the joys of platonic relationships.*

The Commissioners are persuaded that the applicant is likely, if released, to breach the terms of his licence
– *Northern Ireland's Sentence Review Commission on Johnny "Mad Dog" Adair.*

I'm balancing my alcohol and insulin very nicely, thank you
– *How Colin Dexter, creator of Inspector Morse and a diabetic, replies to inquiries about his health.*

The money isn't worth it; it would pay for a carpet perhaps
– *Cameron Pyke, a teacher, on the £500 paid for 100 hours' marking examination papers.*

They were perfectly alert
– *Securicor on its guards who failed to prevent a man attacking Judge Ann Goddard in court.*

I wouldn't be surprised to see this guilt become too much for them. It could lead to suicide
– *Colin Gill, a psychologist, on James*

Bulger's killers, Robert Thompson and Jon Venables, as they prepare for their release with new identities.

Week ending January 20, 2001

But nothing is that funny
– *George Melly, after peering closely at Mick Jagger who had told him that his wrinkles were the result of laughter, not age.*

Is God going to say you paid more so you deserve them?
– *Vickie Allen, who claims that she and her husband had already adopted the twins, advertised for sale on the Internet, who were also adopted by a British couple.*

All that seems to have happened is that these children have been sold to the highest bidder
– *Felicity Collier, head of British Agencies for Adoption and Fostering, on the Internet twins.*

Oh yeah, the guy who came with the runner
– *President-elect George W. Bush, when asked about a meeting last year with William Hague who was accompanied by Sebastian Coe, the Olympic athlete.*

I think the Church of England is finished, dead. I think it will be disestablished and probably join with the free churches and the Methodists
– *Terry Waite.*

I want to succeed in America where, unlike Britain, they do not regard ambition as being the same as eating babies
– *Eddie Izzard*.

Job opportunities for those with earning disabilities
– *Headline in* The Preston Reporter.

I've been poisoned once, I'm not going to be poisoned again
– *A soldier who served in Bosnia when asked if he wants to return there as a reservist.*

He's probably just trying not to get fat
– *Lennox Lewis, the boxing champion, on reports that Mike Tyson is back in training.*

I have never seen an organisation with so many rules, operating standards, instructions, visions and mission statements
– *Sir David Ramsbotham, Chief Inspector of Prisons.*

I don't want a peerage
– *Stuart Wheeler, the betting tycoon who has donated £5 million to the Conservative Party.*

It's the King of England
– *An American seeing Ken Livingstone surrounded by photographers on a walking tour of Harlem.*

Blessed are the young, for they shall inherit the National Debt
– *Sir Malcolm Rifkind, president of the*

Scottish Conservatives, quoting President Herbert Hoover.

If this prosecution succeeds, the days of the pint of beer will be numbered
– *Michael Shrimpton, the barrister representing Steven Thoburn, a grocer being prosecuted for using imperial-only scales.*

The triangular classrooms make a big difference; most of the children can sit in the front row
– *Head teacher of a school that has taken unusual steps to prevent unruly children congregating at the back of the class.*

That will be 26p. Would you like it wrapped?
– *Shop assistant when Rachel Harrison rushed in begging for a chocolate to prevent her diabetic son, four, suffering an attack.*

Week ending January 27, 2001

There is a breakdown in moral values in Peckham and some other areas of London
– *Richard Taylor, father of the murdered schoolboy Damilola.*

I do not accept in any way that I have acted improperly
– *Peter Mandelson announces his resignation.*

I don't think either he or I didn't tell the truth
– *Alastair Campbell on allegations that*

Peter Mandelson had helped the Hinduja brothers' passport application.

Let's hope that you, as an RAF recruit, will be able to be in the front line if you want to
– *William Hague's comment to a schoolgirl, contradicting the Tory policy that women in the front line was "politcal correctness gone mad".*

Winston Churchill, in 1927, described the gentlemen of the City as "the glittering scum which floats upon the deep river of production". There has been something very 1920s about the 1990s
– *Denis MacShane MP.*

Those concerned about the development of deep-vein thrombosis on delayed train and Tube journeys can immediately decrease the risk by giving up their seat to the person standing nearest to them
– *Letter to* The Times.

The references to death are a bit off
– *Hamish Turner, a coroner, on rap star Eminem's lyrics at the inquest of David Hircombe, 17.*

I suppose it wouldn't be most people's choice, really
– *Sir Trevor McDonald on the BBC's decision to move the evening news to 10pm, the same time as ITN.*

There are poems about the Internet and about the shipping forecast but

very few by women celebrating men
– *Germaine Greer addressing the Poetry Society.*

The UK is a nation of immigrants. Immigration is a very good thing and has benefited the country
– *Barbara Roche, Immigration Minister.*

Hippiedom had its great benefits, especially for me. Free love was terrific for about three or four years until women suddenly realised that it wasn't in their interests at all
– *Martin Amis.*

I don't even know my own phone number
– *Chelsea Clinton on the upheaval of leaving the White House.*

We pray particularly that there would be trust, integrity and confidence among them
– *From a prayer for the Shadow Cabinet issued by the Conservative Christian Fellowship.*

Was David's skirt in there?
– *Rubbish collector Mark Oliver's question to Victoria Beckham when rummaging through bags of clothes belonging to the pop star.*

We can't go home. We have got no money to go anywhere. We have no friends left. We are just destitute
– *Judith Kilshaw who appealed against the court decision to take into care the adopted twin babies bought on the Internet.*

Week ending February 3, 2001

Free your mind and your bottom will follow
– *Sarah Ferguson on the secret to weight loss.*

They have pinpointed the jokers in the pack. Now we want the kings
– *Betty Thomas, who lost her granddaughter in the Lockerbie bombing.*

He was curiously detached
– *Alastair Campell on Peter Mandelson's mood after his resignation.*

Try our Mandelson sausages. Full of porkies
– *Sign in the window of a butcher's shop in Richmond, Surrey.*

Every party has a Geoffrey and every party has a Keith. The Geoffreys and Keiths have been around in every regime since Roman times
– *A Cabinet Minister referring to Geoffrey Robinson, the former Paymaster General, and Keith Vaz, Foreign Office Minister.*

Sometimes it's an easy option for a youngster to go into prison for a short time and sit on his bed in his cell doing nothing
– *Lord Woolf, the Lord Chief Justice.*

Over the very long run we see Russia and China as having enormous potential for us. A lot of people with limited means – that's perfect for our concept

– *Anders Dahlvig, group chief executive of Ikea on building an Ikea empire.*

I'm happy but I can't show my happiness when I'm totally exhausted
– *Ellen MacArthur, the British yachtswoman who took the lead in the round-the-world race.*

2.3 quadrillion to one, to the exclusion of everyone on the face of the Earth, now and for ever
– *The odds at which a DNA expert put the chance of a wrong match in the DNA test of a man accused of murdering a British scientist more than 15 years ago.*

It is a marvellous, emotional tale and will appeal to more than just football fans
– *Patrick Nally on producing* Manchester United – The Musical.

The use of natural gravels for facing a building can be an attractive alternative to blocks or bricks
– *Andrew Littler, author of* Sand and Gravel Productions, *responding to Charles Kennedy's reference to "pebble-dash populism" at Prime Minister's Questions.*

Light-hearted banter and horseplay
– *City brokers on an incident where a Jewish trader was told to dress up as Adolf Hitler.*

She wasn't a great speller and she was a messy writer
– *Dr Lynne Vallone who found stories written by Queen Victoria as a child.*

I've met people who have sworn
they've seen God on one substance
or another and I haven't the slightest
doubt they did
– *Martin Sheen who plays the US
President in a television series.*

You need reasonably good sight to be
in the Navy, but as a pilot, once
you've flown a bit you can guess the
way
– *The Duke of York.*

Week ending February 10, 2001

Someone once sent me a marvellous
postcard. It said: "Knock hard. Life is
deaf"
– *Arnold Wesker, the playwright, on his
philosophy.*

My dream was to have a reception in
a marquee, not to be wearing a
marquee
– *Mandy Ruffles, Slimmer of the Year,
who married in August.*

We think it was within the realms of
possibility that it got in there itself
– *RSPCA spokesman on a fox that
strayed into the Houses of Parliament
provoking a hunt throughout the building.*

The rot is setting in and, if unchecked,
will doubtless be regurgitated in
countless PhD theses
– *Sir Donald Sinden on the theory that
Oscar Wilde's* The Importance of
Being Earnest *has a coded homosexual
plot.*

There are 11 bars here, no crèche
and no shop. It would be an ideal
place for a small Waitrose. It could
replace the rifle range
– *Barbara Follett MP on the House of
Commons.*

That's what the whole marriage was
about – lying
– *Patsy Kensit on her union with
estranged husband Liam Gallagher.*

Which end of the train is first class?
– *Remark attributed to Arthur Scargill,
the former miners' leader, on a railway
station.*

The best way to murder anybody in
this country is still to kill them with
a motor car
– *Gwyneth Dunwoody MP calling for
higher penalties for dangerous driving.*

The countryside is not a nice frozen
picture of a Constable painting
– *Ben Gill, president of the National
Farmers' Union in reply to
conservationists who say farming is
destroying the countryside.*

He has asked that people do not call
him sir or bow when they meet him
– *St James's Palace referring to Prince
William.*

It's been like a sauna in here
– *Prince William emerging from the Press
Complaints Commission party.*

There was a kind of liturgy and
choreography that everyone

observed; I think what caused the panic that day was that the choreography was not followed
– *Edward Daly, the priest who tended to a wounded teenager on Bloody Sunday, on that day's events.*

I always dream of the sea
– *Round-the-world sailor Ellen MacArthur after 91 days of the Vendée Globe single-handed yacht race.*

If you like flowers you become a florist and if you like singing and dancing you become a pop star
– *Danny Foster, a member of the pop group chosen on ITV's* Popstars.

Fame is an imprisonment
– *Vanessa Feltz.*

For most people the Church has become little more than a useful landmark by which to offer directions
– *The Archbishop of York.*

Week ending February 17, 2001

It's a sin to be tired
– *Kate Moss, on life in the world of fashion.*

The hardest part was stepping onto dry land
– *Ellen MacArthur.*

The day of the bog-standard comprehensive school is over
– *The Prime Minister's official spokesman.*

It could squeeze all the ingenuity out of them
– *Chairman of the BMA on how doctors might react to reports that compaints about medical incompetence rose by 50 per cent last year.*

Call Falmouth Coastguard we need help – SOS
– *Text message from Rebecca Fyfe, adrift in the Lombok Strait near Bali, to her boyfriend in Britain.*

Driving on a clear day on an open motorway at 80mph is safe
– *Edmund King of the RAC rejects a proposed one-year ban for anyone caught driving over 85mph.*

S★★★! I will call you back
– *Text message from a lorry driver who killed a pedestrian while composing the message.*

You would get a longer sentence if you had a collection of parking tickets stuffed away
– *Michelle Elliott of the charity Kidscape, on sentences imposed on members of a paedophile ring.*

By 2600, the world population would be standing shoulder to shoulder and the electricity consumed would make the earth glow red–hot
– *Professor Stephen Hawking on what would happen if the population continued to increase at its present rate.*

We are fascinated by the darkness in ourselves
– *Sir Anthony Hopkins on his new film, Hannibal.*

It is in remarkably good condition and is the only one we know of
– *Hazel Forsyth of the Museum of London, which put a 17th-century drinking cup in the shape of a penis on display on Valentine's Day.*

They have let us know in advance that they are coming
– *RAF on news that Russian bombers intend to resume patrols of the North.*

What would have happened if it had been a girl stepping out of that helicopter?
– *General Sir Charles Guthrie on women in the Army, referring to the SAS rescue of six British soldiers in Sierra Leone when the first soldier out of the helicopter was killed.*

We had a play together a few weeks ago and it sounded as if we had been playing together for the past 20 years
– *Phil Manzanera, the Roxy Music guitarist, on reforming the band.*

I think my main problem is that I'm not too fat, I'm just too short
– *Brian Hyde-Smith, 21 stone.*

Every boy dreams of being a Bond character
– *Max Reid, who paid £41,125 for the bikini worn by Ursula Andress in* Dr No.

Week ending February 24, 2001

I'm always the last to know anything about fashion
– *Jemima Khan, named best-dressed celebrity at a London Fashion Week ceremony.*

The models were so nervous back stage they were keeping their food down
– *Comedian Jack Dee, compering the Rover British Fashion Awards.*

We know that many of you will take this opportunity to make a significant contribution to party funds in order to secure a second term
– *Invitation to a fundraising dinner sent to Labour-supporting lawyers by the Lord Chancellor.*

Oh God, has he returned? Then there's only one answer – we'll all have to move to New York
– *Literary agent on reports that Salman Rushdie was moving back to London from New York.*

The ratio of mice to men is very low. There's no question of the Queen having to flee to Windsor
– *Buckingham Palace after rodents were seen in the kitchens.*

I am so angry. I would like to see Alan Milburn put on a trolley and made to wait in casualty with just a gown
– *Pensioner Olive Byrne who claims that*

after a 98-hour wait in hospital she was hidden away during a visit by the Health Secretary.

It is quite unusual for people to try to get out of the UK. Most try to get in
– Police officer investigating the body of a stowaway found in the wheel arch of a passenger jet.

France is nice, but it will be difficult to get permission to stay here. We hear we will be treated much better in Britain
– Kurdish asylum seeker speaking on French television.

Stuffy and dusty
– National Audit Office on the Victoria and Albert Museum in London.

If we can't persuade people to visit even the Houses of Parliament, one of the nation's most beautiful and historic buildings, what chance have we got of getting them into the polling booths?
– MP commenting on the failure of the Palace of Westminister to attract visitors.

A diplomat is somebody who can tell you to go to hell and leave you looking forward to the trip
– Alex Salmond, former leader of the Scottish National Party.

The mobile radars weren't destroyed, as the aircraft will find out when they next make a raid
– Tariq Aziz, Iraqi diplomat.

Jerusalem is not built overnight
– Tony Blair telling his party that Labour's 1997 election promises still stand.

I urge everybody not to go on to farms or near farms anywhere in Great Britain at this stage
– Ben Gill, chairman of the National Farmers' Union, on the outbreak of foot-and-mouth disease.

The focus now is not on what we can do for the world but what the workplace can do for you
– Lee Federman, student union president at the London School of Economics.

Week ending March 3, 2001

The only soft drink I can get is water and I don't like water
– Jamie Bell, star of Billy Elliot, *who was too young for a celebratory drink after winning a Bafta award.*

It is dirty, but it is a pig farm. What else could anyone expect?
– Robert Waugh, farmer at the centre of the foot-and-mouth outbreak, replying to criticisms of his farm.

This is the saddest day we have had in 40 years of farming, and we have seen some bad ones
– Joan Brown, whose farm is four miles from the suspected source of the foot-and-mouth outbreak.

No matter how many 8ft hamsters

they sell, the Dome will continue to lose £3 million a month
— Peter Ainsworth, Tory spokesman for culture, media and sport.

Punters are adaptable creatures
— William Hill's bookmakers on news that all horse racing in Britain is to be cancelled.

If we find a British passenger carrying a sausage it will be tested by doctors for the virus
— German Customs spokesman.

It will not be long before there are more lawyers in the country than police officers
— Jack Straw, Home Secretary.

British people are ignorant of good food
— Raymond Blanc, chef.

A good fishfinger butty is hard to beat
— Jamie Oliver, chef.

Don't you think I have given up enough already this year?
— Peter Mandelson, Labour MP, when asked what he would give up for Lent.

If there's a better solo singer in the UK than Craig David, then I'm Margaret Thatcher
— Sir Elton John about the man who lost out at the Brit Awards.

The train's here, it's crashed through my Land Rover

— Gary Hart, whose vehicle careered on to train tracks near Selby, in a 999 call.

He's a pretty charming guy. He put the charm offensive on me and it worked
— President Bush on Tony Blair.

I wanted to be, but I had a few talent problems
— Tony Blair when asked by an inmate at Pentonville Prison if he wanted to be a rock star.

No thanks, I'm thinking
— Keanu Reeves, the actor, declining a couple's invitation to join their table in a New York restaurant.

It is difficult in the beginning to see new faces and learn the names
— Sven-Goran Eriksson, England football manager.

Get it written out in blood
— John Cleese, on negotiating a contract with the BBC.

I never thought the price of getting a tan would be so high
— Anna West, 21, speaking a week before dying from skin cancer.

Richard Blackwood was using the term as it is used in rap music, to mean "woman"
— BBC defending the comedian who referred to the Queen as a "bitch".

Week ending March 10, 2001

We have enough dragons in Wales
— *Siän Lloyd, TV weather forecaster, responding to Anne Robinson's criticism of the Welsh.*

The great thing about us is that we have made us who we are
— *Message from John Diamond, The Times columnist, to his wife, Nigella Lawson, read out at his funeral.*

If a bearded lady had applied we might have had to refuse her as well
— *Waitrose, which rejected a bearded man for a job on hygiene grounds.*

It took us only a day or two to construct but was rather more useful than anything else I wrote while working on networks
— *Quentin Stafford-Fraser, Cambridge computer scientist, on the world's first webcam showing a coffee pot.*

I have only just got to university. I have not had time for these sorts of fun and games
— *Frank Young, 18, who called for the legalisation of cannabis at a Conservative Party conference.*

The Swiss did not say no to Europe. They chose to answer the question later
— *European Commission on the news that the Swiss had rejected membership of the European Union by nearly four to one.*

I arrest you for torture
— *Peter Tatchell, militant campaigner, attempting a citizen's arrest of President Mugabe in Brussels.*

I thought he was joking. He had planned it out and stuff
— *Josh Stevens, American schoolboy whose friend killed two fellow pupils.*

The general theme will be to try to determine what is Yorkshire identity or whether such a thing exists
— *Hull University on its degree in Yorkshire studies.*

Mapmakers have been pinching each other's work for centuries
— *British Cartographic Society.*

Words were exchanged. They were less than civil
— *Scotland Yard on reports that a terrorist who targeted the BBC had a row with another driver before parking his car bomb.*

There was nothing I did which was the cause of the collision
— *Peter Noble, who drank 13 pints before crashing a car and killing six people.*

Brits haven't gone. Nor have we
— *Real IRA graffiti near the Sinn Fein offices in Belfast.*

Sheep know more ways of sickening and dying than any other creature on the planet
— *Germaine Greer.*

I come before you less as an icon of pop and more as an icon of a generation
 Michael Jackson speaking at the Oxford Union.

Moja shamba
— *Swahili for "one garden", the password needed to buy John Le Carré's new novel,* The Constant Gardener, *in Kenya where it is banned.*

I finally feel sexy
— *Jodie Kidd, the model, on putting on two stone.*

Week ending March 17, 2001

I thought I was fit until I did this
— *Charlie Dimmock after 12 weeks training as a trapeze artist.*

These images displayed in the name of art disturb me deeply
— *President of the British Board of Film Classification on Tierney Gearon's photographs of her naked children exhibited in London.*

I don't see sex in any of those prints. If someone else reads that into them, surely that's their issue
— *Tierney Gearon, photographer.*

We would certainly have tried cloning if we hadn't been able to adopt
— *Jilly Cooper.*

You always know you've done well when you're asked back

— *Sting after a party to celebrate the 25th anniversary of the Prince's Trust.*

She saw the police car and believed it was waiting to escort her on her journey
— *Solicitors for the Princess Royal explaining why she drove at 93mph as a patrol car with flashing lights followed her.*

Go away. This evil has come to us from your whore of an England once again ▼
— *French farmer to a British journalist.*

This is going to be a major disease outbreak with a long tail
— *Nick Brown, Agriculture Minister.*

It's not that I'm selling it to spend on binges or snorting cocaine
— *Lord Dalmeny on selling a portrait of*

George Washington to the Smithsonian Institution in Washington for £14 million.

Are you wearing underpants?
— Desmond de Silva QC in court to footballer Lee Bowyer whom he is defending.

Children are being denied trips to the country which are crucial to their development and education
— Margaret Whalley, director of the Youth Hostel Association, which has closed half its hostels as a result of foot-and-mouth disease.

If someone squashes one of those noses near me I could die
— Member of Latex Allergy Support Group on Comic Relief's red noses with latex tongues.

Rear gunners drink lager shandy
— Slogan for a beer advertisement which prompted complaints that it was offensive to homosexual men.

I'm a vulgarian. My taste has always been loud, glitzy and tacky
— Julien Macdonald, the new head designer at Givenchy.

I seek to show that strippers are human beings
— Dr Cathy MacGregor of Nottingham Trent University who plans to dance naked round a pole to analyse a woman's experience of the sex industry.

This is further evidence that people

are coming back to the Conservative Party in leaps and bounds
— Tory spokesman reacting to a report that the party's membership is at a 60-year low.

Since Your Majesty's visit to the Vatican, our nation has passed through difficult times
— Free Presbyterian Church of Scotland blames the Queen for recent floods, train crashes and the outbreak of foot-and-mouth disease.

Week ending March 24, 2001

I used to take my hat off to a single mother. And now that person is me
— Nicole Kidman.

It is a curiously British attitude that says "enjoy yourselves, but not too much"
— Brewers Association on news that pubs are to open for only two extra hours during the Queen's Golden Jubilee.

Every time I return I notice the buzz. I even admire things that don't work well, like the railways and the NHS
— Bill Bryson, the American writer, on Britain.

There has been a multitude of zeros
— West Country shopkeeper on how foot-and-mouth has ruined tourist business.

People standing round holding clipboards and armed with scissors to cut red tape are no help at all
— National Farmers' Union on soldiers

drafted in to help with the foot-and-
mouth outbreak.

Now please cleanse your soles
*– Notice on Devon church beside a
disinfectant footbath.*

They could not spell so I asked if I
could dictate it out loud and write it
as I did so
*– Joanna Trollope explaining in court
why she wrote her own statement instead
of allowing police officers to do so.*

Fifteen years of loyalty; it's the
longest love story of my life
*– Carole Bouquet, actress, after losing a
contract to advertise Chanel.*

It is a problem that goes back to
Agincourt
*– British tour operator alleged to have
broken French employment rules in
Alpine resorts.*

I realised I never wanted to risk my
life again
*– Tracey Edwards, former round-the-world
yacht racer on how having a child
changed her.*

You can achieve more, can get more,
but because of your little minds you
cannot get what you are expected to
get
*– Daniel arap Moi, president of Kenya,
addressing a women's seminar.*

I used to love pushing the spinal cord
out of the middle of the bone and
eating it hot

*– Butcher's assistant in Queniborough
where five died of vCJD.*

Getting arrested is a genius move.
They have never made a tabloid front
page before
*– Pop music insider on the members of
the group S Club 7 arrested for
possessing cannabis.*

We're only human
– A spokesman for The Weakest Link
*TV programme after Anne Robinson
gave the wrong answer to a question.*

Do they do gravestones with Arsenal
on?
*– Mr Justice Laddie on football
merchandise at the trial of a sportswear
trader accused of infringing trademarks.*

When I arrived at the scene I was
short of breath. My chest was tight
and I had blurred vision
*– Richard Parsonson, former policeman,
describes his first incident; he is seeking
£400,000 compensation for stress
working as a traffic patrolman.*

I am Al Gore and I used to be the
next President of the United States
of America
– Al Gore addressing students in Mila

Week ending March 31, 2001

That was Rosie Millard in the Best
Supporting Dress
*– Michael Buerk, the BBC newsreader,
referring to the well-upholstered arts*

correspondent who was covering the
Oscars ceremony.

Sir, you are doing a great job with
that stick, but why don't you sit,
because I may never be here again
— *Julia Roberts, addressing the producer*
who signals to winners to end their
speeches, during her acceptance of the
Oscar for Best Actress for Erin
Brockovich.

Suddenly, going to work tomorrow
doesn't seem like such a good idea
— *Steven Soderbergh after winning the*
Oscar for Best Director for the film
Traffic.

You see, I'm still big over here. Not
anywhere else, but over here
— *Sir Norman Wisdom on his popularity*
in Albania, where his films have been
shown for years.

This is the end of my life's work. It
makes me feel bloody awful
— *Andrew Greenop, a farmer in Renwick,*
watching his healthy sheep being rounded
up to be killed.

If we lose all these sheep it will make
the Exxon Valdez disaster look like a
coffee cup spill
— *David Maclean, MP, on killing a*
unique breed of Lake District sheep
because of foot-and-mouth.

It's like cracking the common cold
— *Tony Blair on the foot-and-mouth*
epidemic.

Sometimes I feel she's an eyeblink
from waking up. It's like when you're
under water close to the surface —
you can see light above you and hear
noises, but you can't break the surface
— *Tony Sandover, whose wife has been in*
a coma for 18 months, on taking her to
Germany for treatment.

The more successful the lead
character is in his sex life, then the
more young people might be
tempted to see some of the many
benefits that come from entering the
profession
— *A Government official on* Teachers, *the*
new Channel 4 drama that has been
condemned as unrealistic by the National
Union of Teachers.

Anyone thinking of going out for a
meal and abusing the staff should
watch out — they could be sitting
next to a table full of police
— *Detective Chief Inspector Brett*
Lovegrove on an undercover operation to
prevent racial harassment in restaurants.

I am not a bad person. Please forgive
me
— *Letter from a teenage girl to a couple on*
whose doorstep she abandoned her baby.

He's a baldy and he has a funny accent
— *Tim Loughton, Conservative spokesman*
for transport, on William Hague.

I seem to be in the right place at the
right time
— *Roger Houlker, a solicitor who has been*

*officially commended for making his
seventh citizen's arrest in 21 years, after
sitting on a man who robbed a woman in
Cheltenham.*

He annoys me enormously, and he
knows he annoys me because I tell
him
– *Sir Paddy Ashdown on the Prime
Minister.*

Week ending April 7, 2001

It was the most liberating experience
of my life, being able to have that
second slice of chocolate cake and
knowing that it is good for the soul
– *Renee Zellweger, who put on two stone
for the film* Bridget Jones's Diary.

My Edward is not gay
– News of the World *headline quoting
the Countess of Wessex.*

Horrid, absolutely horrid, horrid,
horrid
– *Countess of Wessex on Cherie Blair.*

The old dear
– *Countess of Wessex on the Queen.*

There is now "competitive
picnicking" in which families are
trying to outdo each other by
putting on the most lavish spreads
– *A former teacher at Eton, where parents
are asked not to turn the school's fourth of
June celebrations into a display of
corporate hospitality.*

It's not human, not a bear, nor
anything else we have so far been
able to identify
– *Bryan Sykes of the Oxford Institute of
Molecular Medicine on the DNA of a
hair found in Bhutan, believed to be that
of a yeti.*

He's like a bizarre Doppelganger
who walks around doing things
without me
– *Actor Colin Firth on Mr Darcy.*

It's not affected my kitchen. Prices
have fluctuated but it's all becoming
political. And anything political does
my head in
– *Jamie Oliver, the chef, on foot-and-
mouth.*

It's a bit rich coming from someone
who normally goes to Tuscany
– *An MP after Tony Blair's suggestion
that MPs should holiday in Britain to
boost tourism.*

They were just chugging along in
broad daylight
– *Admiral Dennis Blair, US Pacific
Command, on the American spy plane
that made an emergency landing in
China after a mid-air collision.*

Are you ready friends? This is war
– *Message in a Chinese Internet chat
room referring to the US spy plane.*

The key thing here is not to let the
rhetoric get out of hand
– *Ed Rollins, a US Republican Party
strategist.*

We thought we had everything in Italy, but it turns out we lacked one thing: American coffee
– La Stampa, *the Italian newspaper, on the plan by Starbucks to open outlets in Italy.*

I am desperate to give up work
– *Peter Mallet, who won £11.7 million in the lottery.*

Stella doesn't mind what I wear, I've got a clapped-out old farm jacket and she actually nicks it to wear
– *Sir Paul McCartney on his daughter, the fashion designer Stella McCartney.*

He is calm and psychologically strong but exhausted
– *Slobodan Milosevic's lawyer describing his client's condition.*

They think they're going to find a lot of posh dons in strange old buildings
– *John Watts, admissions tutor at Corpus Christi College, Oxford, on why state school sixth formers are failing to apply.*

Week ending April 14, 2001

I am as shallow as a puddle
– *Helen Fielding, creator of Bridget Jones.*

Life for a modern royal is like living in a monastery with glass walls
– *Paul Flynn MP.*

This is the most republican Government since Oliver Cromwell
– *Labour Party adviser.*

He will be profoundly missed by all those people who appreciate wit and unmalicious humour. He was one of the great life-enhancers of our age
– *The Prince of Wales on Harry Secombe, who died aged 79.*

We will win this fight as long as farmers do not intentionally infect their cattle, which we know they are doing
– *Unnamed Army officer on the foot-and-mouth outbreak.*

I feel like Red Marauder: I'm battered and bruised, but still standing
– *Steven Thoburn, the market trader prosecuted for using imperial measures, on winning a £2,500 bet on the Grand National.*

The most famous scales in legal history
– *How a judge referred to the scales used by Steve Thoburn.*

I tried to have a trendy haircut and now I look like a lesbian on the tennis circuit
– *The formerly floppy-haired actor Hugh Grant.*

It's going to be weird to open the fridge and see ourselves staring back at us
– *S Club 7 on signing a deal to promote Pepsi.*

I resolved to be nicer to the wife and kids, to pay them a bit more

attention and not to be quite so grumpy
– Jim Shekhdar on his plans after rowing unaided across the Pacific.

Let's face it, we have always had problems with the English
– Violette Kerivin, 72, a shopper at the Paris branch of Marks & Spencer, which has been told to stay open after failing to consult its staff properly before announcing its closure.

He tipped for the whole British Empire
– New York restaurateur after a British diner left an £11,000 tip.

It's forbidden to be merciful to them, you must give them missiles, with relish – annihilate them
– Ovadia Yosef, spiritual leader of Israel's ultra-Orthodox Shas Party, in a Passover sermon about Arabs.

We're checking for things like dust, bacteria and gases – and to make sure there's not too much hot air
– Dean Cuff, environmental consultant, on checking air quality in the House of Commons.

Congratulations. You didn't turn this into a crisis
– President Bush to his foreign policy team as the American aircrew, which had been held in China, touched down on Guam.

Any person (except players) caught collecting golf balls on this course

will be prosecuted and have their balls removed
– Notice beside the first tee at Spey Bay Golf Club, Moray.

Week ending April 21, 2001

As an elf you have to be so erect and centred
– Liv Tyler on working in the film The Lord of the Rings.

Patients need less pain-relieving medication, they are better patients, and they need to stay in hospital for a shorter period of time
– New NHS leaflet on the expected benefits of planting trees around hospitals.

It was a typical instinctive response from someone who believed in right and wrong
– Peter Sherlock on his wife Liz, who was killed trying to prevent thieves stealing her handbag in London.

Her manner has been described as that of a dominatrix, but with her practical cropped hair and glasses, she is more like a school librarian in a black leather coat. Her insults are innocuous
– The New York Times on Anne Robinson's The Weakest Link.

Redheads may possess genes passed down from Neanderthals
– Researchers at Oxford on the trail of the ginger gene say it is older than homo sapiens.

Please, no more bank holidays. We have enough cold, damp, miserable days as it is
– *Letter to* The Times.

The Lord told me I no longer needed car insurance. Instead he would bless me with his divine protection
– *Peter David in court facing motoring charges.*

I have come to realise the sheer terrorism of the fashion industry
– *Liz Jones, former* Marie Claire *editor, on the backlash against her campaign to ban super-thin models from women's magazines.*

With his death goes the truth. I don't know whether he'd ever talk about it, but I'm not for getting rid of the evidence
– *Kathy Wilburn, who lost two grandchildren in the Oklahoma City bomb, on why Timothy McVeigh should not be executed.*

People are asking if they can sell T-shirts and buttons. We have no control over what they sell. We just ask that it is in good taste
– *Judith Anderson, mayor of Terre Haute, Indiana, on preparations for McVeigh's execution.*

They were gormless. But there was an innocence in the gormlessness
– *Andy Kershaw on his erstwhile Radio 1 colleagues.*

The handgun business is a dying business
– *The editor of* American Handgunner *magazine referring to steeply declining sales.*

You expect too much from us
– *Arsène Wenger to Arsenal fans after his team lost 3–0 to bottom-of-the-league Middlesbrough.*

He needs someone to be there 100 per cent of the time. He thinks that's love. That's not love. That's babysitting
– *Jane Fonda explains why she has filed for divorce from Ted Turner after ten years of marriage.*

Week ending April 28, 2001

I found it interesting and very fictional
– *Cherie Blair on a novel by Susan Crosland about an unprincipled and power-crazed Prime Minister.*

I don't think I will do a Mafia character again. I want to get away from the violence. It is starting to bother me
– *James Gandolfini, of the TV series* The Sopranos.

This generously funded and largely unaccountable body devotes its energies to stigmatising the white majority population and stirring up resentment among Britain's black and Asian minorities
– *Raj Chandran on the Commission for*

Racial Equality, of which he was formerly a member.

The way to improve relations would be for immigrant organisations to express gratitude to the English for allowing them the inestimable privilege of living in this civilised country, whose superiority to their own explains their pressures to colonise it
– *Sir Alfred Sherman.*

Bogus asylum seekers? Conservatives reduced the number before. We will do so again
– *A Conservative Association advertisement in former Home Secretary Michael Howard's local paper, the* Folkestone Herald.

Not very optimum
– *Peter Grossenbacher, of Swiss Rail, on Britain's railway system*

Boy George is all England needs: another queen who can't dress
– *Joan Rivers.*

Many people do take pride in being English, but the idea of discussing English nationalism is, in polite circles, rather like talking about an embarrassing itch
– *St George's Day comment by Gavin Esler, TV presenter.*

An extra public holiday to mark Nelson's victory at Trafalgar? Will it be backdated?
– *Letter to* The Times.

Visitors will realise *Fawlty Towers* was really a documentary
– *New* Lonely Planet *travel guide on British hotels.*

We are confident with our security procedures
– *Ministry of Defence on reports that 30 electronic listening devices were found in its offices.*

The argument about spoiling views would not mean very much to most Londoners
– *Ken Livingstone, London mayor, who believes tall buildings are more useful than the views they block.*

In what language do you think?
– *Question on the Swiss census form.*

We do not serve chicken tikka masala. Our chefs would not know how to make it
– *Iqbal Wahhab, who has opened two Indian restaurants in London.*

Nothing tastes quite like a gerbil; they are small and tasty to eat; morsels of sweet rodent protein, from whiskers to cute little feet
– *Start of a poem by Tony Langham, deemed by Leeds City Council "not suitable material to be sent to schools".*

Hasim, you know it was a lucky punch
– *Lennox Lewis after being knocked out by Hasim Rahman.*

The vicar's wife has to get on with everyone, but you can take only so

much of hearing that the sun shines out of your husband's bum
– *Susan Devonshire-Jones, a vicar's wife.*

Some people are old at 35 because they are blasé about the world. I am blasé about nothing
– *Charles Aznavour, 76.*

Being an artist seems to absolve a person from accepting responsibility. If a record doesn't sell, it's the record company's fault. If a concert flops, it's the promoter's fault
– *John Reid, Sir Elton John's former manager.*

All writing is a campaign against cliché
– *Martin Amis.*

As far as men go, I've had two major loves in my life and that's enough
– *Actress Charlotte Rampling.*

I cut it mainly to relieve me of the bondage of self
– *Jennifer Aniston, the actress, on her new hair style.*

I have the best wife for the line of work that I'm in. She doesn't try to steal the limelight
– *George W. Bush.*

Week ending May 5, 2001

You've all got umbrellas
– *Zara Phillips complaining to the media at her first royal charitable engagement, which took place in the rain.*

It is vital that the politically correct and race relations gestapo do not stop these issues being discussed
– *John Townend MP.*

The only black guy I ever saw in Tory Central Office was the doorman. He was my great hope for a while, but now even he has gone
– *Lord Taylor of Warwick.*

Besides being out of work, to my mind I'd lost one of the greatest jobs in the world
– *Sir Paul McCartney on the period after the Beatles split up.*

It's like the NSPCC having a paedophile as its patron
– *Angela Walder, a senior member of the RSPCA, on having the Queen, who supports foxhunting, as the society's patron.*

There is a picture of confusion, bewilderment and ignorance about the European Union among Britons
– *An official in Brussels on the results of a European poll on the EU.*

A sea of yellow fluorescent jackets
– *Assistant Commissioner Mike Todd on the police presence during the May Day protests.*

Monopoly mayhem
– *Anti-capitalism demonstrators on their protest.*

What's a poor girl to do when she's

against globalisation but needs a new frock?
– *A shopper in Oxford Street, London, during the May Day protests.*

It gives a whole new meaning to the phrase "a vision for Britain"
– *Tony Blair on his new spectacles.*

People are just getting older
– *Jane Root, controller of BBC2, on commissioning three comedy series about divorce and mid-life crises.*

Marriage vows should be written like a dog's licence that has to be renewed every year
– *Rod Stewart.*

How are your feet?
– *The Queen after knighting Sir Steven Redgrave, who ran the London Marathon.*

I love space. It was a great trip here
– *American "space tourist" Dennis Tito's first words to the astronaunts at the space station.*

The college is 500 years old, but it is safe to say that was a unique event
– *A fellow of Magdalene College, Cambridge, on the South African scholar who performed a tribal dance saluting Nelson Mandela during a university ceremony.*

Garden conservation has gathered to itself the moss of sterility
– *Sir Roy Strong.*

Examiners are dispassionate, but if you succeed in infiltrating one semi-colon into an essay, they will be so filled with nostalgic delight that a pass grade is assured
– *Eric Dehn, of Bristol, advising A-level candidates in a letter to* The Times.

My last wish is to walk into a Margate pub and buy a pint of bitter
– *Ronnie Biggs, the Great Train Robber, who wants to return to Britain after more than 35 years on the run.*

Week ending May 12, 2001

I've had a big chip on my shoulder all my life. I've still got it but now it's not weighing me down
– *Tracey Emin, artist.*

You'd hear a cow roaring to a calf, or you might hear a lot of sheep and think, "Oh crumbs, they are getting out." This is going to be a year without landmarks
– *Layland Branfield, a Dartmoor farmer whose stock was culled.*

My hair has turned grey and I have lost even more on top
– *Ben Gill, president of the National Farmers' Union.*

I feel rather sorry for the chap. He was a fine figure of a man, a lady's man, but now he seems senile
– *Malcolm Fewtrell, 91, the detective who caught Ronnie Biggs, the Great Train robber, in 1963.*

Most people have a dream. This is ours
– David Barnden, chosen with his wife to farm the remote Bardsey Island off North Wales.

It is intended to send out the message that we admire girlie swots
– Labour party aide on the choice of St Saviour's and St Olave's School to launch the general election campaign.

They know that if they take time off they are going to have to give up their life's work
– Professor Nancy Lane on reports that women with degrees in technology are least likely to marry.

They are not delighted. There has been much furrowing of brows. It seems that nothing is sacred any more
– Royal adviser on the Queen having to miss a day's racing at Ascot for the State Opening of Parliament on June 20.

It should be a ritual of reflection on guilt and forgiving and the recognition that life must go on
– Gerhard Monninger, a German Protestant minister advocating a Church ritual for divorce.

The more attractive a man is, the more chance he gets to destroy his first marriage. Tallness is pretty universally attractive, I don't know why
– Dr Allan Mazur on findings that tall men are more likely to commit adultery.

When people choose a sexual partner they are making an unconscious attempt to relive a past conflict or loss, to deal with something that happened in childhood or in the past
– Marcia Millman, a Professor of Sociology in California.

I was going round and round and kept hitting things. I remember wondering if I could hold my breath
– Pamela Steward, 72, who was sucked under a car ferry when her yacht capsized.

We apologise for the lack of scenery
– Announcement on a Connex train stuck in a tunnel in Sussex.

This boy has a sense of justice
– Gore Vidal on Timothy McVeigh, the Oklahoma City bomber.

I once raced a helicopter in a Jaguar along there. You can do it in ten minutes if you really cane it, but you tend to hit a few sheep
– Jeremy Clarkson on his favourite road, Buttertubs Pass in Yorkshire.

Week ending May 19, 2001

Britney backs Blair
– The slogan beneath a picture of Britney Spears reported to have been hanging in pride of place at Labour's headquarters in Millbank, London.

They go on about law and order but

if they don't mind stealing our posters they can't be that big on crime
– *Amy Utton, who had her anti-Tory banner removed before the arrival of William Hague and a walkabout in Portsmouth city centre.*

He should learn judo, it would be much quicker
– *William Hague, the Tory leader, on Deputy Prime Minister John Prescott's punch at a protester in Rhyl, North Wales.*

I can set John Prescott up with a trainer and I will guarantee he will become British champion within five fights
– *Frank Maloney, co-manager of former world champion Lennox Lewis.*

I hope we can get back to campaigning on real issues without any violence or intimidation
– *John Prescott.*

She murdered him in life and tried to murder him again in death by trying to ruin his reputation
– *Detective Chief Inspector Jim Dickie on Jane Andrews, former aide to the Duchess of York, who was convicted of the murder of her lover Tommy Cressman.*

We need someone with more faith than the Pope
– *Advertisement for a knife-thrower's assistant for the Cottle and Austen Circus.*

Don't try to be charming or witty, or debonair. Just be yourself
– *George W. Bush, recounting the advice of his wife, Laura.*

How not to do my make-up
– *Bianca Jagger, when asked what she learnt from Andy Warhol.*

It needs to be someone with a sensible sense of loonyism
– *Alan Hope, leader of the Monster Raving Loony Party, which is seeking a candidate for Harrow.*

While undoubtedly committing a crime, the interest was a healthy one
– *James Prowse, a district judge, on a 13-year-old boy on trial for dealing in child pornography.*

I could not fail Sarah, like everyone else had. She is now at rest
– *James Lawson, the father who helped his daughter, who suffered from depression, to die.*

It's better than getting pregnant without a husband
– *One of the five wives of Tom Green, a Mormon charged in Utah with polygamy.*

My favourite drink is squash. I'm very dehydrated and I'll pay you for it
– *Matthew Head calling out to children listening for owls 11 days after he became trapped in a mineshaft in Somerset.*

They do have some holes and a rip

and they're faded. But I have a pair of jeans that look much worse
— *American auctioneer on the oldest known pair of Levi's jeans which date from the 1880s.*

Don't be silly. Go away
— *Unnamed cashier at Romsey station, Hampshire, confronted by a balaclava-clad gunman demanding money. He fled empty-handed.*

Week ending May 26, 2001

They last longer than rock stars
— *Jerry Hall, ex-wife of Mick Jagger, on why she prefers diamonds to husbands.*

There is no reason why pupils cannot be examined all day. Schools can start examinations earlier in the morning and let them go on later in the afternoon
— *George Turnbull, of the AQA exam board, on timetables which subject some pupils to eight hours of exams in a day.*

I have spoken to people who have been threatened and others who have alleged a murder and a kidnapping linked to cricket corruption
— *Lord Condon.*

It probably makes him more aerodynamic
— *Sir Tom Finney, 79, former England football star on David Beckham's Mohawk haircut.*

Call now before you get egg on your face

— *Advertisement by the British Association of Anger Management.*

If you are like me you won't necessarily remember everything you did here. Now that can be a good thing . . .
— *President George W. Bush, accepting an honorary degree at Yale University.*

I was told my arrival here was unexpected. But I passed the cinema and found you were expecting me after all. The billboards read *The Mummy Returns*
— *Margaret Thatcher addressing an election rally in Plymouth.*

I didn't realise the whole family were here
— *The Queen when viewing a display of creepers, spiders and strangely shaped vegetables at the Chelsea Flower Show.*

People simply do not want chrome designs which resemble their office to relax in
— *Robin Williams, chairman of the Chelsea Flower Show, on accusations that the judges discriminated against modernist garden designs.*

Sorry, but they are coming to shoot you
— *Laura Barron, five, telling her pet sheep and its day-old lamb that they have to be culled because of foot-and-mouth disease.*

I prefer men with more hair
— *Jo Balchin, a student who ruffled Tony*

Blair's hair when he visited her college in Southampton.

It won't make a big difference. Most people know who won the war
— *Disney on cuts to its film* Pearl Harbor *for Japanese audiences.*

There would have been a great deal of humiliation if he had been beaten by a corn-fed piece of poultry
— *Brett Capaldi, whose greyhound beat a pigeon in a race.*

Week ending June 2, 2001

She doesn't need a dressing down, she needs a dressing up
— *Nigel de Gruchy, teachers' union leader, on Lisa "Penny" Ellis, a teacher and* Big Brother *contestant, who has appeared naked twice on TV.*

We believe it was an accident when Penny dropped her towel twice
— *Channel 4 on footage which it did not edit out of its* Big Brother *programme.*

Sex? Certainly not, never in my books will there be explicit sex
— *Ann Widdecombe promoting her novel at the Hay-on-Wye literary festival.*

We could have gone faster but we wanted to arrive in Marseilles for the 8pm news
— *Drivers of a new high-speed train that covered the 672 miles between Calais and Marseilles in a world-record time of 3hr 20min.*

I have played every one of these holes in my head throughout the years
— *Bill Clinton during a round of golf on the Old Course at St Andrews.*

Hair matters. This is a life lesson Wellesley and Yale Law School failed to instil. Your hair will send significant messages to those around you
— *Hillary Clinton to students.*

Some people ding and dong in the wrong place, and I would prefer bell ringing, but this is wonderful
— *The Rev Norman Lea of St Catwg's in Cadoxton, Vale of Glamorgan, whose parishoners have to imitate bell ringing because of a lack of ringers.*

You have to do much the same thing as we are trying to do here
— *President Thabo Mbeki of South Africa on how to prevent race riots such as those in Oldham.*

Following England has to be the way ahead
— *Nasser Hussain, England cricket captain, calls on British Pakistanis to support England against Pakistan at Old Trafford.*

What were you doing on September 9, 1986? Could it be possible you were having dinner with me here — will you do that?
— *Words alleged by the prosecution to have been spoken by Lord Archer to persuade a friend to give him an alibi.*

The first thing we did was look at old James Bond movies
— *US Army spokesman on its new $1 million armoured car equipped with gadgets such as a spinning laser gun and electric door handles.*

I don't mind whether it's art or not. It is to me
— *Martin Creed, whose crumpled sheet of A4 paper was shortlisted for the Turner Prize.*

I am drawn to the possibility of downloading a man
— *Marilene Oliver, an art student who has photographed the dismembered body of an American murderer executed in 1993 and reconstructed it on life-sized sheets.*

Nobody in our family can drink. We have a chemical imbalance
— *Tony Booth, father of Cherie Blair.*

If it was just one woman I might worry. But all women adore him
— *Lady Connery, wife of Sean.*

Week ending June 9, 2001

I prefer direct campaigning, like protesting outside the rubbish incinerator in Edmonton. I'm not standing there for fun. It's very smelly
— *Julia Stephenson, a Green Party candidate.*

There was an accidental burst of fire from an automatic weapon
— *Nepalese royal family source on the Crown Prince's shooting of his father, mother and six relatives.*

If they are relaxed they are more likely to remember things
— *David Oakley, of University College London, on teaching students self-hypnosis techniques to help them pass exams.*

d:*O WUCIWUG ONo:-VTE LBR 2MORO
— *Text message from the Labour Party to mobile phones. The first few digits are a sideways picture of William Hague, the rest reads: "What you see is what you get. Oh no! Vote Labour tomorrow."*

My hair is a bit like the Tory Party: there is nothing you can do with it
— *Tony Blair.*

The only freedom you have is to put the cross in that box. As soon as you do that, you've signed it away
— *Leonard Cruickshank, a community leader in Liverpool.*

It's all about whether or not we can move the Royle family off their sofa
— *Labour strategist on apathy among Labour voters.*

I have colleagues who believe that if you see a car with four black kids it is worth giving it a pull because at least two of them are up to no good
— *Asian police officer on racism within the force.*

I stood under the shower for what seemed like an hour and since then I have been drinking endless cups of tea
— *David Chell, released after three years on death row in Malaysia.*

Some see me as a tragic heroine, and that's what makes me acceptable to them. The idea that I might be happy is unforgivable
— *Domestic goddess Nigella Lawson, whose mother, husband and sister all died from cancer.*

I have always relished the idea of my work being not simply misunderstood by readers, but also comprehensively misinterpreted by the professionals
— *Will Self, novelist.*

Everyone has trousers and hardly anyone has chainsaws
— *Royal Society for the Prevention of Accidents on why there were nearly 6,000 accidents last year involving people getting dressed, five times the number of injuries caused by chainsaws.*

Sink drains are a metaphor for the unknown. The freeing of blockages is like the freeing of people
— *A curator explains a lavatory plunger on a pedestal at the Venice Biennale art exhibition.*

My sister watches you after the racing
— *Princess Margaret to Richard Whiteley, the TV personality.*

I knew I'd conquered America when Mike Tyson told me I was one mean lady
— *Anne Robinson on taking* The Weakest Link *quiz show to the United States.*

Week ending June 16, 2001

It really spoilt my night
— *Los Angeles fire service employee rung by distraught fans after rumours that Britney Spears had been killed in a car accident.*

If I don't practise I am going to destroy this language
— *President George W. Bush after an interview in Spanish.*

As I face an uncertain future, the white suit will be more necessary than ever
— *Martin Bell, former BBC war correspondent and defeated independent MP.*

I am an unashamed and unrepentant doggie person
— *Gerry Adams.*

When she reads out the Ten Commandments at Westminster Cathedral it sounds as though she has written them herself
— *Father Michael Seed on Ann Widdecombe.*

He loses his temper on Monday and doesn't find it again until Friday
— *A civil servant on John Prescott, the Deputy Prime Minister.*

Have you gone yet?
– *The Prince of Wales to actress Amanda Barrie, whose character Alma Halliwell in* Coronation Street *is dying.*

Do you mind going to the hotel? Then I can get my guests back
– *Harrogate bride Rebecca Garnett to former President Bill Clinton who visited her wedding reception.*

It was like a holiday camp. They had their own beds and three modest meals
– *Czelaw Geborski, accused of murdering German women in Poland after the war, interrupting a witness describing the horrors of camp life.*

It allows them to think for themselves
– *Bernice McCabe, head teacher, on replacing A levels with the international baccalaureate.*

We are not amused at the lack of seriousness
– *Tunisian United Nations envoy on a British attempt to ease negotiations with music.*

The odd £1,000 would have made a lot of difference to some of the people who looked after her
– *A friend of the late Christine Van Gulik who lived on handouts from friends despite her secret £12 million fortune.*

Now there are 169 people dead
– *Anti-death-penalty poster at the*

execution of Timothy McVeigh who killed 168 people in Oklahoma.

When was the last time someone was killed by a conker?
– *Jenny Richards, a mother of three, in Norwich where horse chestnut trees are to be felled in "the interests of public safety".*

Sad people devote more energy to work to distract themselves from their sad feelings
– *Dr Robert Sinclair, psychologist, on why sad people make better workers.*

It was a joke. We called it hunt the photographs
– *Lord Archer's former secretary on how staff had to find pictures of his wife, removed from the walls of the Archers' flat by Andrina Colquhoun, his mistress.*

This is my first trip to Brussels as Foreign Secretary for the United Kingdom
– *Jack Straw, speaking in Luxembourg.*

Week ending June 23, 2001

I don't turn round to Victoria and say, "Good morning, I'm an icon"
– *David Beckham, after* The Face *magazine published new pictures of him battered and bleeding tomato ketchup from his head.*

I am not irresponsible. We are in a better position to bring up children than a couple of drug addicts

– 62-year-old French woman who gave birth to her brother's baby in order to secure an heir to their 80-year-old mother's £2 million fortune.

Tell us your date of birth and we can work it out
– The judge in Lord Archer's trial trying to get Andrina Colquhoun, Archer's former mistress, to admit her age in court.

Ho Chi Minh City is as good a place as anywhere to contemplate the future of the Conservative Party leadership
– Kenneth Clarke, former Chancellor, on a business trip to Vietnam.

It is bonkers to say that being bald is a factor in whether you can be a leader. Half the presidents of France have been bald
– Iain Duncan Smith.

A very sad day for the sport
– Alec Stewart, the England cricket captain, after Pakistan fans invaded the pitch during the NatWest series.

I thought it was a parking fine because it was the same sort of envelope. I opened it quickly before my husband saw it because I thought I would be getting some points on my driving licence
– Christine James, formerly the tennis star Christine Truman, on receiving notification of her MBE.

I couldn't get her off so I sank my teeth into her neck. She let go ▼
– A woman, 73, who bit a pit bull dog that attacked her terrier.

Perhaps it is idealistic to suppose that any minister might know their

subject, but a passing interest is not beyond expectations
– *Clare Balding, BBC sports presenter, on the lamentable performance of Richard Caborn, the new Minister for Sport, in her live sports quiz.*

They were so big and aggressive-looking that none of our engineers wanted to go near them
– *Michael Copp, a BT health and safety officer, on a cluster of poisonous spiders found living beneath Windsor Castle.*

I've told her that it's called *The Geneva Monologues* and that it's about women in banking
– *Maureen Lipman on telling her mother about her role in the West End show* The Vagina Monologues.

I think she ate just one pea
– *Gordon House, head of BBC radio drama, on taking Calista Flockhart, star of the television programme* Ally McBeal, *out to dinner.*

There is no margin for error and the hairs stand up on the back of my neck
– *A 747 pilot on how he feels when landing at Heathrow because it is so busy. The Civil Aviation Authority admitted that there is one emergency each day at the airport.*

Week ending June 30, 2001

I did have him on the ropes
– *Barry Cowan, ranked 265th in world*

tennis, who became the first Briton to take Pete Sampras to a fifth set at Wimbledon.

No matter where they go, someone is out there waiting
– *Denise Fergus, mother of James Bulger, on the release of her son's killers.*

We should all take a deep breath
– *David Blunkett, Home Secretary, appealing for calm after vigilantes promised to track down the Bulger killers.*

We don't really know what to call her but I think a shebra is the favourite
– *Karen Peet, who runs an animal park in Cumbria, on a foal with a Shetland pony mother and a zebra father.*

The "save the pound" election was as big a disaster for us as "ban the bomb" was for the Labour Party
– *Kenneth Clarke, announcing his candidature for the Conservative Party leadership.*

Ken is the only one of the leadership candidates who really worries us. He is the only one who looks more or less like a human being
– *Labour strategist.*

Michael used to use his quiff as a symbol of right-wing virility. Now he has settled for a parting and he is greying at the temples
– *A colleague of Michael Portillo on his bid for the Tory leadership.*

I feel hurt. This is totally unfair. I am the best DJ in Britain and I have worked my guts out for these people. Now they repay me with this
— *Chris Evans, sacked from Virgin for drinking in a pub after saying he was too ill to work.*

We never get photographed when we're gardening together or baking cakes
— *Billie Piper, Evans' wife.*

He was saved because he was a bouncing baby
— *Orthopaedic registrar David Hartwright, on two-year-old Job Robinson, who fell 30ft from a window and suffered only minor bruising.*

I wasn't really thinking about getting scratched, just about holding on
— *Jo Lobb, 21, the falconer who captured Foster, an escaped vulture.*

It was to see how people would respond if I died
— *President Fidel Castro of Cuba joking on television after fainting at the podium during a marathon speech.*

I put my hands up saying, "There is no trouble here." Then an officer lifted his riot shield and smashed it in my face
— *Shahid Malik, a member of the Government's race relations watchdog, beaten and arrested trying to prevent a confrontation between police and Asians in Burnley.*

Week ending July 7, 2001

When other little girls wanted to be ballet dancers, I wanted to be a vampire
— *Actress Angelina Jolie, who plays Lara Croft.*

They are surprised at what some of the words mean
— *Paul Gibson, a teacher at a Cornish school where children are encouraged to explore swear words in an attempt to stop bad language.*

Many parents I know ask their children to smoke — if they are going to — at home so they don't get caught
— *Mo Mowlam calls for the legalisation of cannabis.*

We've sold our Sol to the devil
— *Spurs fan on the transfer of Sol Campbell to Arsenal.*

Why you did it will never be known
— *Mr Justice Gage, summing up in the trial of Barry George, convicted of murdering Jill Dando on her doorstep.*

The police were like fathers to him and when anything happened he called 999. He didn't have anybody else to talk to
— *Itsuko Toide, ex-wife of Barry George.*

The 07.38 is cancelled today owing to non-cervical stock
— *Announcement by Thameslink at St Albans station.*

Are you having fun? I can't tell, you're being so polite
— *Madonna to the audience during her concert in London.*

It was rather like a game of Monopoly
— *Ted Francis on being taken around London and shown or given money by Lord Archer.*

He's working. First one I ever had who did
— *Joan Collins on why she attended a charity launch without her boyfriend, theatre director Percy Gibson.*

I'm always interested in meeting new men. You can call me Available Albright
— *Madeleine Albright, 64, Former US Secretary of State.*

It's being taken along with Ecstasy by clubbers. I have no idea what effect that has
— *Detective Sergeant Roger Moxey of the Heathrow crime squad on the theft of five drums of Viagra.*

I did not feel my best, but I did not let it show. I kept clutching my red Hermes bag, which matched my red hat and red jacket. Chic colour co-ordination counts even in an emergency
— *Princess Michael of Kent after a helicopter emergency landing on a mountain in Peru.*

I consider this tribunal false tribunal and indictments false indictments
— *Slobodan Milosevic on trial in The Hague.*

I thought I was going to melt into my shoes
— *A visitor to Henley Royal Regatta where men had to wear their blazers despite the heat.*

dad@hvn, urspshl.we want wot u want@urth2b like hvn.giv us food&4giv r sins lyk we 4giv uvaz.don't test us!save us!bcos we kno ur boss, ur tuf&ur cool 4 eva!ok?
— *Text message translation of the Lord's Prayer; part of a scheme to send church services to worshippers on their mobile phones.*

Week ending July 14, 2001

We are richer than anyone else in this street because we are constantly expanding our minds
— *Deborah Bee, a squatter in a £3 million home in North London.*

We wouldn't do anything like that with the future King of England
— *Jenny Frost from the pop group Atomic Kitten referring to Geri Halliwell's pinching the Prince of Wales's bottom.*

Water cannon would have cleared the road in an hour
— *Marsha Singh, Labour MP for Bradford West, on the need for tougher measures against rioters.*

I don't care now if I never win a match in my life again. This is it
– *Goran Ivanisevic after winning the Wimbledon men's final.*

Pinochet will remain in history as having been spared a trial because he is insane
– *A prosecution lawyer after a Chilean court ruled that the former dictator was unfit to stand trial.*

It's pot, it's all-female shortlists, and it's opposing Section 28
– *An opponent of Michael Portillo lists the issues that he felt would cost the Shadow Chancellor the race for leadership of the Tory party. This list was refined by another MP to "Weed, women and woofters".*

Intransparent to consumers, rigid and at levels unrelated to the cost of carriage
– *European Commission on the high cost of international mobile phone calls.*

There is room for an adult intelligent debate
– *David Blunkett, Home Secretary, hints at the possibility of legalising cannabis.*

Swilling 14 pints of lager constitutes a far greater social threat than a shared joint
– *Ian McEwan, novelist.*

This is only the fifth time I have worn it and the elastic has gone already
– *A shareholder on her dress while criticising the board of Marks & Spencer, which announced a fall in sales of its clothes.*

Running the rail industry has become *Who Wants to be a Millionaire?* with every entrant a winner
– *Mick Rix, leader of the train drivers' union, on the Railtrack chief's £50,000 pay rise, his second since October.*

I regret the extra stresses put on students and teachers
– *Estelle Morris, Education Minister, apologises for the AS level shambles.*

Fat soldiers upset the "Bunters-wehr"
– *Headline in* The Times *reporting on obesity problems in the German armed forces.*

There is one-upmanship to buy the latest models, which are given pride of place in the home
– *Wendy Rogers from Tesco on competition between the young male owners of irons.*

WKND
– *Text message abbreviation for "Weekend" now recognised by Oxford Dictionaries.*

Week ending July 21, 2001

It's eerie down there. It feels like you're out in the universe
–*Yasemin Dalkilic, who smashed her own world freediving record plunging*

105 metres into the Red Sea with one gulp of air.

I would just get in their way
– *Michael Portillo bows out of the Tory leadership ballot.*

She was neat
– *President George W. Bush on the Queen.*

This could be the Las Vegas of Europe
– *Blackpool businessman welcomes proposals to ease restrictions on gambling.*

There's enough trouble with muggings and pickpockets without the mafia, guns and goodness knows what
– *A Blackpudlian on the proposals.*

It was the most embarrassing situation
– *An Oxford police officer after raiders padlocked police gates and went on to raid a bank.*

What will Phillip Morris argue next: that we should put people down at 50 because it would save money on healthcare?
– *British Lung Foundation on a suggestion from the tobacco company that its products boost national economies by killing smokers early.*

God took two of them and he gave us seven
– *Fahad Qahtani, father of septuplets; two of his previous children died.*

It is as if Genoa has been hit by a killer virus and the authorities are trying to isolate the epidemic
– Corriere della Sera, *the Italian newspaper, on the extravagant security precautions surrounding the G8 summit.*

Oxford was right to reject me. I didn't deserve to get in
– *Laura Spence, now studying at Harvard, who was turned down by Magdalen College, Oxford.*

I think he will handle it well. He might write a book about it
– *Michael Crick, biographer of Jeffrey Archer, on how the disgraced Tory grandee might cope with prison life.*

He's very frightening
– *The Duchess of York on the Duke of Edinburgh.*

If U do it again U will be cut off
– *Text message from West Midlands fire officers to malicious callers on mobiles to try to reduce hoax calls.*

If you put the patient at the heart of medicine then Bristol would never have happened
– *Dr Stephen Boisin who raised the alarm about baby deaths at Bristol Royal Infirmary.*

Could Bristol happen again? Could it be happening right now? The honest answer is that it could
– *Professor Kennedy, chairman of the inquiry.*

Week ending July 28, 2001

Give me macho, or give me death
– *Madonna on men.*

She does not like to be kept waiting
by people, especially her own
security
– *Spokesman for Madonna who sacked a
security man who had gone out for a
takeaway meal.*

What career?
– *Roger Moore, the James Bond Star,
when asked if a tribute lunch in his
honour marked the end of his career.*

They interpret any noise louder than
a boo as criticism
– *Gwyneth Dunwoody, Labour MP, on
the Government.*

Even if it has come off the front
pages of the newspapers, it has not
gone away
– *The Prince of Wales on foot-and-mouth
disease.*

Few of our customers have to wear
suits to work. They will be for their
first interview or first court
appearance
– *David Shepherd, a director of Top Man
menswear.*

This is a bad time to be graduating,
to be in your fifties, to be in debt or
to be in power
– *Patience Wheatcroft writing in* The
Times *about economic recession.*

There is far too much meaningless
drivel and sloppy, emotive, over-
romantic description
– *Food Standards Agency on food
labelling.*

Slow down. The sea isn't going to
evaporate
– *Signs on French autoroutes to the
Mediterranean.*

Probably the most comprehensive
and difficult agreement in human
history
– *New Zealand representative on
adoption of Kyoto protocol to tackle global
warming.*

Cockroaches of the seas
– *Senior official of Japan's Fisheries
Agency on minke whales.*

This wasn't a vote, it was an auction
and Japan was the highest bidder
– *Conservationist on failure of proposals
to create anti-whaling havens.*

They made a whispering noise as
they went past and I was thinking, "Is
it really something which could kill
me?" It was such a gentle sound
– *British tourist caught in the Sri Lanka
airport gun battle.*

Unfortunately it is all true. In fact it
was worse
– *A Genoese policeman confirms
accusations of police brutality during the
G8 summit to* La Repubblica *newspaper.*

Genoa will serve as an example for future summits. We have nothing to reproach ourselves about
– *Gianni De Genaro, head of Italian police, rejects international condemnation.*

The world has gone mad
– *Tony Blair complains that the media paid more attention to the protests in Genoa than to the G8 discussions.*

It has been appalling; passengers deserve better
– *Head of Connex South Eastern train company on the past two years' service.*

I am not hugely important. I am hugely self-important
– *Andrew Marr, political editor of the BBC.*

Week ending August 4, 2001

It is acting in its purest form, because you know what Michael Caine said about films: you act with your eyes
– *Helena Bonham Carter on playing a chimpanzee, with only her eyes visible, in the new film* Planet of the Apes.

This is a sad day for all of us in Britain who work for good race relations
– *Lord Janner, vice-president of the World Jewish Congress, on the High Court decision to admit the black Islamic leader Louis Farrakhan to Britain.*

You speak good sense and someone should make you king one day
– *Boris Johnson on the Prince of Wales's views on rural life.*

Insects can be gay, with males routinely copulating with each other
– *Buckingham University vice-chancellor on an article called "A Note on the Apparent Lowering of Moral Standards in the Lepidoptera".*

These guys are playing jokes. I am here and suddenly I am the worst thing ever. Nato have to look at everything they did. I didn't do anything wrong. They did
– *Slobodan Milosevic.*

What sort of military force would we have if, each time there was an injury, the injured party sued his senior officer for negligence?
– *Simon Weston, Falklands veteran, on a proposal that police should sue for injuries during the riots in Bradford.*

We have all had a drink at 10 o'clock in the morning. There is no reason why we should be forbidden from doing so, provided that we are not making a din
– *Kenneth Clarke.*

Almost anybody you have ever heard of, I was his deputy
– *Lord Hattersley on his career.*

You have to conjure up some serious powers of imagination to find any of the actresses in the series even remotely sexy
– *Kyle MacLachlan, the actor, on his* Sex in the City *co-stars.*

If this is considered acceptable material then we are tearing down all the barriers of decency on television
– *Tessa Jowell, Secretary of State for Culture, on a spoof documentary about paedophilia shown on Channel 4.*

I practise in front of the mirror saying, "Hi, I'm Julia. I'm single"
– *Actress Julia Roberts on starting to date again.*

She is a law unto herself and takes no notice
– *Aide on the Queen Mother's refusal to follow advice from the Queen and Prince Charles.*

Ministers agree only that, whatever happens, there should never be a public inquiry
– *Simon Jenkins, in* The Times, *criticises the handling of the foot-and-mouth epidemic.*

I note that you have a window box attached to the outside of your flat. For safety reasons I am afraid I have to ask you to move it
– *Letter from Norwich City Council, which had prieviously tried to cut down chestnut trees to prevent children endangering themselves by collecting conkers.*

Week ending August 11, 2001

I am really looking forward to my wedding day; I can't wait to meet my husband
– *Joke by comedian Shazia Mirza, the self-proclaimed "first Muslim woman in the history of stand-up".*

With a human it's different
– *Severino Antinori, the Italian embryologist, while dismissing objectors to human cloning as "vets".*

It is overkill. I don't think people can consume all the matches that are now on offer
– *Commentator John Motson on plans for more televised football.*

A lot of agricultural reformers would want farmers to stand around being subsidised and making thatched roofs. Well, that's for the birds
– *Lord Haskins, Rural Recovery co-ordinator.*

Builder's bum is one of Britain's great institutions
– *Frank Douglas, a builder, on Amec's ban on "bum cleavage".*

This is a country in which if you're old you become invisible. People notice you only if you're taking up too much time at the supermarket checkout, or if you fall over in the street. The same is true if you are a writer
– *Francis King, novelist.*

It would be better to stay in my own country because I would be killed because of my aims, not because of nothing
– *Davoud Rasul Naseri, an Iranian*

asylum-seeker in Glasgow, after being stabbed.

Wouldn't it be nice if Jesus lived in England
– *Paraphrase of the song* Jerusalem *by a Stockport vicar who banned it from a wedding ceremony as too nationalistic.*

We expect it when we see it, there is no deadline
– *Bloomsbury, the publishing firm, on reports that J. K. Rowling's fifth Harry novel was delayed by writer's block.*

To the untrained human ear it sounds like a pant, a "huh, huh" ▼
– *Patricia Simonet, an American scientist, who claims that dogs laugh.*

A rare species on the Fringe: a show that exceeds its own blurb

– The Scotsman *reviewing a Japanese production of* Medea *at the Edinburgh Festival.*

Beyond fat cats
– *The RAC on BP's £5.58 billion profits in the first half of this year.*

I don't need it, but I want it
– *Sir Paul McCartney, prevented by his fiancée Heather Mills from salvaging a cupboard from a skip.*

She was petulant, aggressive and confrontational. She elected to turn up five hours late and, of course, she never apologised. The room was packed with sycophants laughing at her every word and plying her with praise and organic salad
– *Vanessa Feltz on an interview with Madonna.*

IT WASN'T ME WHO LAUGHED – IT WAS THE DOG

Week ending August 18, 2001

The most stupid, ill-educated and nasty woman can rubbish the nicest, kindest and most intelligent man and no one protests
– *Doris Lessing on sexism against men.*

An old person, fond of animals and having briefly seen WWF being used in wrestling, might decide to donate to the RSPCA instead
– *Judge Justice Jacobs ruling that the initials WWF belong to the World Wide Fund for Nature, not the World Wrestling Federation.*

Nonsense on stilts
– *Christine Hamilton on sexual assault allegations against her and her husband.*

I sometimes think farmers are a pretty ungrateful lot
– *Elliot Morley, Agriculture Minister.*

Children with the first-day cover will find friends peering over their shoulders, which will lead to an avalanche of interest
– *Stanley Gibbons, stamp dealers, on new scratch-and-sniff stamps.*

Weeds can be good. Untidy gardening is not a bad thing. Nettles are excellent
– *The RSPB urges people not to deprive wildlife of habitats by sanitising gardens.*

I wish people would see playing fields as outdoor classrooms. Then they would be more outraged
– *Gyles Brandreth, vice-president of the National Playing Fields Association, on the sale of school land to developers.*

There are perks to being flat-chested. I can pass for 14 in a blackout
– *Jenny Eclair, the comedian, performing at the Edinburgh Festival.*

It would not be effective in an urban environment
– *Tony Harman, of a pest control company, on foxhunting with hounds.*

Art is dragging him around on a leash and he doesn't know it
– *Damien Hirst, the artist, on Charles Saatchi, the art collector.*

People who refuse to take holidays, claiming pressure of work, are petty, insecure and heading for a breakdown
– *Nicholas Coleridge, managing director of Condé Nast Magazines.*

He looked stunned, but when he saw the money he agreed
– *John Fashanu, the footballer-turned TV presenter, who paid a tramp £300 to queue on his behalf overnight to buy a London flat.*

Exams are getting more girly
– *Ruth Lea, Institute of Directors, on why female pupils do better at A level.*

Language came as easily as breathing for 50 years, and I can't do it any more. It is indescribable
– *William Manchester, unable to finish his biography of Churchill.*

Are doctors prepared to pay £10 to patients when they are not seen at their appointed time?
– *Letter to* The Times *on a proposal to charge patients £10 for missing appointments.*

The Queen accepts she has to sort out the relationship between Charles and Camilla, and that means to smile on a marriage
– The Spectator.

Week ending August 25, 2001

When I first watched *Enigma* I was, like, why on earth didn't anyone just tell me to stop eating
– *Kate Winslet, after losing four stone, on her latest film.*

The question of why this policeman was not prosecuted is really a matter for the police
– *A Government spokesman on Detective Superintendent Adrian Roberts, who was not prosecuted because he claimed he could not remember who was driving his car when it was photographed breaking the speed limit.*

Four of my friends have got through. I have tried three times
– *Afghan asylum-seeker at the Sangatte refugee centre, Calais.*

I don't really care where it is going
– *Beatrice Muller, 82, who lives on the* QE2 *because it is cheaper than staying in an old people's home in America.*

Scotland? I'll buy you Scotland
– *Jeffrey Archer to Richard Cohen, who edited several of his novels.*

They hardly ever missed school and rarely suffered from coughs and colds
– *Professor David Wolke on bullies.*

I politely asked the audience to use the break for further coughing
– *Andras Schiff, the pianist, who interrupted a recital in Edinburgh because of coughing, sneezing and mobile phones ringing.*

That's spot on, absolutely. I think almost everything I have done since I was 35 has been a disaster, hasn't it?
– *John Cleese, when asked if he was "a one-joke comedian".*

Duchess would be too grand. Lady too common. Countess is the perfect compromise.
– *Buckingham Palace insider on what title Camilla Parker Bowles would receive on marriage to the Prince of Wales.*

I do not understand how Ken Clarke could lead today's Conservative Party to anything other than disaster
– *Margaret Thatcher.*

The Conservative Party has had quite enough of people throwing their toys out of the pram
– *Kenneth Clarke.*

For the protection of future rape victims, I urge both the Hamiltons

and Nadine Milroy-Sloan to shut up
— *Norman Brennan, director of the*
Victims of Crime Trust.

When I was a GP, I owed my sanity
to the breathing spaces provided by
unkept appointments
— *Dr Kenneth Mole in a letter to* The
Times.

I write about people who have been
dead for 200 years and eat the
occasional fried egg
— *Dame Beryl Bainbridge.*

Week ending September 1, 2001

Handsome men are usually arrogant,
and beautiful women are horribly
insecure
— *Actress Fiona Fullerton.*

They keep saying on television that
he was killed. He wasn't. He was
murdered
— *Kevin Collins, father of Sapper Ian*
Collins who was killed in Macedonia
when a concrete block was dropped onto
his Land Rover.

There isn't enough food, water or
medicine and we don't know what
we are going to do with all these
people. We are worried about what
they will do to us
— *Crew member of the* Tampa, *which*
rescued 438 Afghan boat people and was
then stranded off Australia amid an
international row over which country
should take them.

Keep out
— *Headline in the* Herald Sun,
Melbourne, declares that 96 per cent of
Australians back their government's
refusal to admit the Tampa *refugees.*

We should stop thinking of older
people as problems and acknowledge
that most of them have solved more
problems than we've had hot
breakfasts
— *Richard Holloway, former Bishop of*
Edinburgh.

I've only been in England for an
hour and I wish I hadn't come
— *Australian woman tourist stranded at*
Stansted airport by the lack of public
transport after midnight.

The writer Doris Lessing thinks men
are having a hard time. It's about
time. They are still not being
murdered by their spouses
— *Germaine Greer.*

I can be a real pain in the neck
— *Rolf Harris.*

The sight of a child's pushchair on
the lawn at Parham is worth £5 on
the ticket price
— *Simon Jenkins,* The Times *columnist,*
urging the National Trust to encourage
ancestral families to live in stately homes
open to the public.

I'm not a banana
— *Christine Hamilton who said, before*
police dismissed allegations of sexual

assault, that if the claims could be proved she was a banana.

If I were to ask you what it is like to be a member of the Royal Family, you wouldn't have a clue. It is just by an accident of birth, a cross we have to bear
– *The Duke of York.*

Young women know the difference between literature and popular fiction. We know the difference between foie gras and Hula Hoops; sometimes we want Hula Hoops
– *Jenny Colgan, author and comedian, defending "chick-lit" writers.*

If you can't have fun as an ageing sex symbol when you hit 60, I don't know what will become of you
– *Raquel Welch, 60.*

When you have an individual in some type of a crisis, yelling for her to jump is insensitive
– *A Seattle police officer on drivers who heckled a woman threatening to throw herself from a road bridge. She jumped – and survived.*

Week ending September 8, 2001

I'm a jobbing writer, like everyone else
– *Fay Weldon on why she agreed to write a product-placement novel commissioned by a jewellery company.*

Don't mention the score
– *Headline in the* News of the World

and Independent on Sunday *reporting England's 5–1 football defeat of Germany.*

It is more than a defeat, it is a national disgrace, quite unbelievable
– *German newspaper* BZ *laments the result.*

Nothing out here is worth a British soldier dying for
– *Andy Taylor, Parachute Regiment captain, on Macedonia.*

I am ashamed to be a loyalist today
– *Billy Hutchinson, a convicted UVF terrorist, after attacks on Catholic children and parents walking to school in Belfast.*

Jim and I are both communicating constantly and Mia remains the happy child that she always has been
– *Kate Winslet explains her marriage split.*

We are steering clear of any sentimental marriage imitations. There will be no flowers, no confetti and no declaration of vows
– *Alexander Cannell, half of Britain's first gay couple to register their partnership in a civil ceremony.*

This fight is bigger than life itself
– *Don King, the boxing promoter, talks up the heavyweight title rematch between Britain's Lennox Lewis and Hasim Rahman, of America.*

Nearly vanquished
– *Cardinal Cormac Murphy-O'Connor on Christianity in Britain.*

This has caused only a small ball of fire and does not blow the car up
— *BMW after the new Mini was recalled over fears that vapour from the fuel tank could explode.*

We seized the sporran because it contained animal hair and posed a risk to Australia
— *Quarantine officials on why they impounded a traditional piece of Celtic clothing imported for a wedding in Melbourne.*

Would you give your right arm to know why sharks attack; could it be revenge? Go vegetarian
— *Billboard slogan used by the animal rights group Peta, and withdrawn after two fatal shark attacks in the United States.*

You are more likely to get killed by a falling coconut than killed by a shark
— *Elizabeth Downey of the London Aquarium.*

There is a rather short list of ways whereby this condition can arise
— *Nasa on the possibility that astronauts on the International Space Station might get pregnant.*

It's quite delicious, actually
— *Merryn Dineley, brewer of a recreated neolithic ale flavoured with cow dung.*

England very good . . . France no good
— *Ahmed, a Kurd, explains why he is one of the hundreds besieging the Channel Tunnel.*

Week ending September 15, 2001

We have been attacked like we haven't since Pearl Harbor
— *Admiral Robert J. Natter, commander of the US Atlantic Fleet at the Norfolk navy base on the September 11 terrorism.*

We are now on Delta [imminent threat], the whole world is on Delta
— *American official describing an upgrade to the highest level of preparedness.*

I'm traumatised for life. Someone needs to take responsibility for this. This was somebody's father, this was somebody's sister, somebody's mother. We should have seen this coming. I'm disgusted
— *Clemant Lewin, who saw people jumping from as high as the 80th floor of the World Trade Center, including a man and woman holding hands as they fell.*

There are over 300 doctors here and they have been divided up into four trauma teams
— *Dr Luis Marcos, president of New York Health and Hospitals Corporation*

The number of casualties will be more than any of us can bear, ultimately
— *Rudolph Giuliani, Mayor of New York.*

I was appalled to learn of the terrible tragedies across the United States. The scale of the carnage and suffering is truly devastating. My thoughts, prayers and sympathies are

with all those caught up in these horrific events
– *The Archbishop of Canterbury.*

I send my condolences to the President, the Government and the people for this terrible incident. We are completely shocked. It's unbelievable
– *Yassir Arafat, Palestinian leader.*

My Government condemns these terrorist attacks to the utmost
– *Gerhard Schröder, the German Chancellor.*

Italy is at the side of the United States
– *President Ciampi of Italy.*

The United States of America is face-to-face with one of the greatest tragedies in its history, something that could affect the entire world
– *Bulent Ecevit, Turkish Prime Minister.*

This terrorism is dangerous and we denounce terrorism. We denounce terrorism under any circumstances
– *President Mubarak of Egypt.*

What should I tell the pilot?
– *Last words spoken by Barbara Olson, calling her husband on a mobile phone from United Airlines flight 175 just before it crashed into the Pentagon.*

Terrorist attacks can shake the foundations of our biggest buildings, but they cannot touch the foundation of America. These acts

shattered steel, but cannot dent the steel of American resolve
– *President George W. Bush.*

The American cowboy is reaping the fruits of his crimes against humanity
– *Iraqi state television.*

We're all gonna die, but three of us are going to do something. I love you, honey
– *Tom Burnett, a Californian businessman, in a phone call to his wife from the jet that crashed near Pittsburgh.*

We have more planes, we have other planes
– *Hijacker overheard by air traffic controllers.*

We're dying
– *A stockbroker answering the phone in the offices of Cantor Fitzgerald, near the top of the World Trade Center.*

He looked in real good shape for a guy who fell from the 83rd floor
– *Bronx firefighter on a policeman pulled from the rubble with only cuts to his hands and face.*

They seemed more concerned that their sister might break a nail than they might themselves win the US Open
– *Alix Ramsay in* The Times *on the tennis final between Venus and Serena Williams.*

It is still a big issue
– *John Bird, co-founder of the* Big Issue,

on homelessness as the magazine
celebrated its tenth birthday.

I'm becoming a bit of a computer
whiz
— *Harry Fishwick, former mill worker,
who made medical history when all eight
of his fingers were sewn back on after an
accident.*

Shearer is Owen's John the Baptist.
He prepared the way for the team we
have now
— *David Shenton, a Leicestershire vicar,
on the England football side.*

He was pretty good
— *Mark Folland, 19, who lent Tony Blair
his guitar during a visit to Hartlepool.*

Blair is regarded by most people in
Britain as a smarmy git
— *Paddy Ashdown.*

I didn't think to dial 999
— *Mark Ashton-Smith, a university
lecturer, who rang his father in Dubai
when his kayak capsized in the Solent.*

A haven for gun-toting crackpots
— *The opinion of Mike Parker, a travel
writer, on rural Wales and its English
immigrants.*

Suits are a definite no-no
— *Guide for Young Conservatives trying
to recruit university freshers this month.*

You are a fornicating adulterer. You
disgust me
— *Simon Waddington, who confronted a*

vicar during a church service about the
vicar's affair with his wife.

The Law Society is full of
champagne-sipping racists
— *Kamlesh Bahl, former vice-president of
the Law Society.*

Week ending September 22, 2001

There will be a series of battles. They
will be fought visibly sometimes, and
sometimes we'll never see what is
taking place
— *President George W. Bush warns
Americans that the war on terrorism will
be long.*

I am not a pacifist like my son. I
believe in an eye for an eye. Turning
the other cheek will not stop these
barbarians. Every mother who has
lost a child will feel the same. I hope
Bush is the man he says he is
— *Pauline Berkeley, of Shrewsbury, whose
son Graham was killed on Flight 175,
the second plane to hit the World Trade
Center on September 11.*

I am convinced that military action
will not prevent further acts of
international terrorism against the
United States
— *Barbara Lee, a Democratic
congresswoman.*

No invading force has ever tamed
Afghanistan. Even Alexander the
Great
— *Colonel Yuri Malishev, a Red Army
veteran who took part in the Soviet*

Union's abortive invasion of Afghanistan in the 1980s.

We are in for a long campaign but if we don't win it then I think that the consequences could be catastrophic
– Tony Blair.

The enemies of our country look on us as a thorn in their eye and seek different excuses to finish us off. Osama bin Laden is one of these excuses
– Mullah Mohammed Omar, the Taleban leader.

Iain's problem is that however nicely he says it, his message attracts these people
– Steve Norris, former vice-chairman of the Conservative Party, on the appeal of Iain Duncan Smith, the new party leader, to extremists.

There is too much breathlessness about the world of espionage and intelligence and I wanted to bring it down to something normal
– Dame Stella Rimington, former head of MI5, explaining why she wrote her controversial memoirs.

The last time I tried to make a bed, I broke two ribs
– Dame Muriel Spark, 83.

I wouldn't say I was dishonest, but there have been times when I haven't been totally truthful
– Nick Leeson, the rogue City trader.

You are, whatever you say, every parent's nightmare
– Judge Selwood of Portsmouth Crown Court sentencing 34-year-old Paul Tramontini, a teacher, to 18 months in prison for eloping with a 15-year-old pupil.

Chirac is a hunter of hearts. The presence of a husband hardly bothers him. He has known, in the biblical sense, actresses, Italian and otherwise, journalists, women about whom it is flattering to be said to be the lover
– Extract from the memoirs of Jean-Claude Lomond, former chauffeur to the French President.

Hello, I'm Sir Denis Thatcher. Who are you? Are you very, very famous?
– Thatcher on meeting Lady Victoria Hervey, the "It" girl.

Week ending September 29, 2001

America has no truer friend than Great Britain. Once again we are joined together in a great cause
– President George W. Bush.

You cannot imagine what it is like to be descibed as a terrorist, and a dead man, when you are innocent and alive
– Saeed Al-Ghamid, a pilot with Saudi Arabian Airlines. His name was used by one of the American attackers, leading to his being wrongfully accused of involvement in the hijackings.

They are extraordinary creatures. They are working as hard as anyone on the site and at the day's end you can see they are totally exhausted. But you can bet they'll be back 12 hours later, raring to go again
– A policeman at the site of the collapsed World Trade Center praises the rescue dogs, many of which are said to be suffering from depression as a result of not finding any survivors.

Operation Enduring Freedom
– New codename for the American offensive against terrorism, changed from Operation Infinite Justice for fear of offending innocent Muslims.

Today we must firmly declare that the Cold War is over. The world is at a new stage
– Vladimir Putin, President of Russia.

It will get easier as time goes on. Everyone will get bored with me
– Prince William on his new life as a university undergraduate.

Why is Posh writing a book of her memoirs? She can't even chew gum and walk in a straight line at the same time
– Liam Gallagher of Oasis on Victoria Beckham.

With all these problems that keep piling up, we may find ourselves serving vacuum-packed food. Then all we would have to do is cut a bag open, empty the meal on to a plate and say "Bon appetit"

– Bernard Taligrot, a French restaurateur, on the shortage of qualified chefs in France.

I'd have loved to have played every part. I'd have been brilliant
– Mick Jagger talks about Enigma, *the first film from his production company Jagged Films.*

If I ever get to do my musical I want to do it with two legs, not one
– Claire Sweeney of Brookside *on why she refused to swim through a crocodile-infested swamp as part of her* Challenge of a Lifetime *television programme.*

I asked the barmaid for a quickie. I was mortified when the man next to me said, "It's pronounced quiche"
– Luigi Amaduzzi, the Italian ambassador, on the pitfalls of trying to speak a foreign language.

If your wife has an account at the bank, Patrice Chopin will not only take care of her money. Her intimacy interests him as well
– A neon sign displayed in a Parisian pet shop by a husband denouncing his wife's lover, who is a banker.

Week ending October 6, 2001

I am sick of it. I just don't care any more
– Calista Flockhart on her TV role as Ally McBeal.

The sternest and most detailed threat

yet of imminent military attacks on the Taleban
– The Wall Street Journal *on Tony Blair's speech at the Labour Party conference.*

Without Brown there would be no Blair
– GQ *magazine, whose readers voted Gordon Brown as the most influential man in Britain.*

Stolidarity
– *John Prescott, the Deputy Prime Minister, coins a word when describing the commitment required in the campaign against terrorism.*

Humour is like any other useful tool. It has its time and its place. You wouldn't fix a watch with a hammer and I'm not going to bring Osama bin Laden to his knees with quips and puns
– *P. J. O'Rourke, American satirist.*

They are to produce a protective bubble of positive energy and bombard the terrorists with white light and love from our higher selves
– *Description by actress Shirley MacLaine of her "chakra meditation sessions".*

If you can't rely on the Swiss, who can you rely on?
– *Richard Sutton, a passenger stranded when Swissair collapsed.*

This row about Prince William being filmed going into lectures would

never have happened in my day. Art students never went to lectures
– *Eamonn Butler of the Adam Smith Institute.*

Some of my friends cannot talk. They are just raving idiots
– *Jamie Oliver, the "Naked Chef".*

I hate McDonald's. I can't think of anything I hate more than McDonald's apart from Pot Noodle
– *Sir Terence Conran.*

Is your bull male or female?
– *Reply from an official at the Department of Food and Rural Affairs to an inquiry by the wife of a Monmouthshire farmer.*

Someone asked what keeps me awake at night. I said, "My husband, I'm glad to say." This man said, "You mean snoring?" I said, "No, I do not mean snoring." I was a bit cross about being misunderstood
– *Prunella Scales, the actress, and wife of Timothy West.*

British universities are on the verge of going bankrupt so we desperately need money now, not decades down the road
– *Andrew Oswald, Professor of Economics at Warwick University, on proposals to scrap tuition fees and introduce a graduate tax instead.*

If Rolf Harris seems to have been with us for ever, that's because he has been
– *From the dustjacket of his autobiography.*

I love him so much. He is the poet who haunts me more than anyone else. There is nobody like him. I think we're joined at the hip
– *Andrew Motion, the Poet Laureate, on John Keats.*

Week ending October 13, 2001

My assignment was not a stupid stunt. I travelled more than 60 miles in Afghanistan and wandered around and observed
– *British newspaper reporter Yvonne Ridley after being released by the Taleban.*

Londonistan
– *Sobriquet given to the British capital by French intelligence because so many suspected members of al-Qaeda visit it.*

The Arab and Muslim voices of reason have been overshadowed by the war cries of the fanatics
– The Yemen Times.

Policy bible
– *Whitehall shorthand title for briefing paper designed to reassure Muslim and Arab states that hostilities will not spread beyond Afghanistan.*

The Americans must know there are thousands of young people who are as keen about death as Americans are about life
– *Sulaiman Abu Ghaith, spokesman for al-Qaeda.*

What we are defending cannot be defined simply in terms of borders and frontiers. We are now defending values, certain things we believe about our way of life, our freedom, our ability to respect people of different faiths, persuasions and creeds
– *Tony Blair addressing British soldiers in Oman.*

Mr Blair has become America's chief foreign ambassador to members of the emerging coalition against Osama bin Laden
– The Wall Street Journal.

In the current state of global anxiety, could you publish a map showing the whereabouts of the moral high ground?
– *Letter to* The Times.

I know it's the male menopause but I fancy a 500cc Kawasaki
– *Sir Paul Nurse on how he hopes to spend the money from his Nobel Prize for Medicine.*

It's now a very good day to get out anything we want to bury. Councillors' expenses?
– *Memo from Jo Moore, adviser to Stephen Byers, Secretary of State for Trade and Industry, sent an hour after the September 11 attacks on New York.*

The truth is that women are better drivers
– *Admiral Insurance Services after the Advertising Standards Authority had*

rejected complaints about an advertisement featuring that claim.

You must all have had trouble getting a literate secretary who knows where to put commas and full stops. With anyone under the age of 45 it is almost impossible
– Professor Graham Zellick, vice-chancellor of the University of London.

I play Roxanne and I have one scene when I'm locked in a fencing fight with nothing but a corset and stockings on
– Joan Collins on her first appearance on the British stage for a decade.

I can't wait to open a magazine and see myself
– Beyonce Knowels, singer with Destiny's Child, anticipates her launch as the new face of L'Oreal.

Week ending October 20, 2001

All my life I have sneered at the old farts who said the world is going to the dogs and at last I have realised, my God, they are right
– Jan Morris, travel writer.

We turn levers and get clean water, push a button for hot coffee, open doors and get ice-cream, take short car trips to places where planes wait before whisking us across continents as we nap. Is it possible that we are being given a last great gift before everything changes?
– Peggy Noonan, former speech writer to

Presidents Reagan and Bush Sr, writing in 1998, predicts terrorist attacks on America.

I am no good at marriage, but I love men. I have spent most of my life pleasing them, and now I am going to please myself
– Joan Collins.

What's your brother up to these days?
– The Prince of Wales on meeting Bakr bin Laden, brother of Osama.

At times like this the media and a lot of men go mad. It's all those toys they played with when they were children
– Clare Short, International Development Secretary.

My writing is like fine wine; the more you read, the more you get from it. Reading it once is like taking a dog to the theatre
– V. S. Naipaul, winner of the Nobel Prize for Literature.

While driving my wife and her mother on a fraught journey, I was forced to ask my wife: "Who is driving this car, you or your mother?"
– Letter to The Times.

The sight of Tony Blair and George Bush running around like cowboys makes me want to weep
– Doris Lessing.

America and Britain will never track down my father. He's now in the safest place in the world
– *Abdullah, son of Osama bin Laden.*

Women simply cannot limit themselves to less than ten conversational topics
– *Professor Petra Boynton of University College London on findings that women have a broader range of conversational topics than men.*

Get back to your salads
– *A diet guru urges New Yorkers not to neglect their waistlines.*

It is a question of who are we Australians that Ned Kelly should be our greatest hero?
– *Peter Carey on the protagonist of his Booker prizewinning novel.*

Residents of Anthrax Street, in Fayetteville, North Carolina, want to change its name
– The Times *reporting on "anthrax anxiety" in the United States.*

More people have been struck by lightning in the past ten days, I bet, than have contracted anthrax. The country badly needs to settle down
– *John McCain, US Senator.*

Pub-goers everywhere other than Lancashire are having their money creamed off, like the froth on top of a pint
– *The editor of* The Good Pub Guide

on beer prices and profiteering by some breweries.

Week ending October 27, 2001

Psychiatry is a waste of good couches. Why should I make a psychiatrist laugh, and then pay him?
– *Kathy Lette, novelist.*

Self-knowledge does not necessarily help a novelist. It helps a human being a great deal but novelists are often appalling human beings
– *Peter Carey.*

They want people with cute faces and cute bottoms and nothing else in between
– *Reporter Kate Adie when asked about the alleged dumbing down of television.*

When two or more television presenters are gathered together, and the subject of Anne Robinson comes up, the air grows green and acrid with spite and envy
– *Esther Rantzen.*

Are you seriously going to transcribe all this? But Lynn! You could be shopping!
– *Anne Robinson after being interviewed by Lynn Barber.*

She's about as cuddly as a cornered ferret
– *Lynn Barber on Anne Robinson.*

The way John Humphrys' mind

works is a mystery to many of us
– *Jeremy Paxman.*

Peace man!
– *Headline in* The Sun *greets the simultaneous decriminalisation of cannabis and decommissioning of a few IRA weapons.*

We have now witnessed an event in which the IRA has put a quantity of ams completely beyond use
– *General John de Chastelain.*

The lesson of history is that the worst way of preparing a country for a crisis is to suppress arguments
– *Michael Dobbs, novelist.*

The trouble with people like you is that you are so clever with words that us up North cannot answer back
– *Government Chief Whip Hilary Armstrong to Labour MP Paul Marsden.*

Please ensure if you intend using talcum powder that any spillage or residue is cleared after use. Failure to do so may result in a security incident
– *Notice to staff at the House of Commons during the anthrax scare.*

Dogs used to be the worst thing we worried about in this job
– *Washington postal worker, ditto.*

They are proven to be tough warriors. I am a bit surprised at how doggedly they're hanging on

– *Spokesman admits that the Pentagon had underestimated the Taleban soldiers.*

I am past writing angst songs for kids. My angst is when I can't get my Porsche roof up and when I can't get my golf handicap down
– *Alice Cooper, rock star.*

Would the sample which should have been sent to the laboratory of the Government Chemist be discovered at the back of the fridge in some dark corner of the Institute for Animal Health?
– *Defra minister Margaret Beckett explains to Parliament that BSE research scientists have tested the wrong animal brains.*

Week ending November 3, 2001

The very phrase "British film industry" depresses me. I don't think we've got a film industry, and never have had. We've been making bloody awful films
– *Emma Thompson, actress.*

My choice does not reflect any lack of commitment to English cricket
– *Andy Caddick, pace bowler, on his decision not to join England's tour of India.*

There's not heather growing between people's ears
– *Willie McSporran, on the residents of Gigha who united to buy their island.*

We go out dressed up as cats, drink a few bottles of wine, then throw flour and eggs at each other ... Later we eat a Mars bar out of a boy's pants
— *Rhiannon Evans describing the initiation rituals of Alley Catz, a Cambridge University women's drinking society.*

Drinking was never a problem until I needed a new liver
— *Larry Hagman, actor.*

When they got hit with a wee, fat, balding, working-class, ex-communist, Celtic-supporting British Unionist they take a wee bit of time to figure it out
— *John Reid on the reactions to himself in Northern Ireland.*

People ask "Can they fly?"
— *Shaun Bridges, craftsman, facing a rush for his willow broomsticks, due to Harry Pottermania.*

Tallybin
— *John Prescott conflates Taleban and bin Laden for the benefit of the House of Commons.*

The bombardment of Afghanistan has put the al-Qaeda network in a "win–win" situation
— *Sir Michael Howard, military historian.*

Don't get depressed that something terrible is going to happen; we shouldn't let something like that ruin our enjoyment of the city

— *Ken Livingstone, mayor of London, urges its inhabitants to get out more.*

I seek the indulgence of the House
— *Michael Martin, Speaker of the House of Commons after breaking the convention of impartiality.*

Now it's the wrong sort of electricity
— *Overheard on a train after news that Connex's 55 new trains cannot run because "they use power in a fundamentally different way".*

He had a great rapport with himself
— *Russ Abbot on the late Tommy Cooper, his fellow comedian.*

Ninety-nine per cent of people would have reacted the way I did
— *Tony Martin, the farmer whose murder conviction for shooting an intruder was reduced to manslaughter.*

If one were going to be interviewed by anyone, it wouldn't be you
— *The Queen to John Humphrys of Radio 4's* Today *programme.*

It is like kissing the Berlin Wall
— *Helena Bonham Carter on acting with Woody Allen.*

Week ending November 10, 2001

You would have to live in a cave not to have heard of Harry Potter
— *Cher, following her attendance at the film's world premiere.*

When I took the role in Harry Potter, my kids sat me down and told

me I had better be careful to get my character right. They warned me that kids would write and let me know if I wasn't successful. Boy, talk about pressure
— *Robbie Coltrane, actor.*

There were more people in church than I have had in a long time
— *The Rev Tony Tooby on being attacked by young Muslim vandals in his Bradford church.*

He lost count of his children, but fathered at least seven sons
— *Obituary of Roy Boulting, the British film-maker.*

The Dickensian idea of reasonable chastisement has no place in a modern civilised society
— *Mary Marsh, director of the NSPCC, on the Government's decision not to outlaw parents smacking their children.*

Barry will be revered by those he would want to be revered by
— *Carla Lane on Barry Horne, the jailed animal rights protester who died on hunger strike.*

Great for us who are slightly out of shape
— *A customer applauds the return of Marks & Spencer to its classic clothing ranges.*

When I look at these works, "culture" only makes me think of yoghurt

— *Edna Weiss, Royal Academician, on the Turner Prize shortlist.*

Dads unable to be there at bathtime or bedtime should phone to say goodnight and make up for it the next morning at breakfast
— *Dr Howard Steele, who claims that babies deprived of paternal contact in the first year of life often develop antisocial traits.*

It's pretty unlikely he would have approved the showing of his teeth to people
— *Director of George Washington's Virginia estate on the decision to display his dentures in an attempt to attract visitors.*

Do me a favour, spend a lot of money
— *Rudolph Giuliani, the mayor of New York, greets the passengers of BA's first Concorde flight since the Paris crash.*

No group should in future have privileged hereditary access to the Lords
— *Lord Williams of Mostyn, leader of the House of Lords.*

The rats had got at it
— *Paul Tyler MP on the Government's proposals to reform the House of Lords*

People who go to the polar regions are statistically less likely to die than salesmen who drive on motorways in England
— *Sir Ranulph Fiennes, explorer*

For me, England is the most exotic place in the world: the British manners, the stratification of society. You see it even in people's shoes
– *Henri Cartier-Bresson, photographer.*

An actress friend said she'd married a Fascist and a Marxist; neither of them took the garbage out
– *Gloria Steinem, feminist.*

Week ending November 17, 2001

As I read the news this morning it was like a dream
– *Jamila Mujahid, a Radio Afghanistan presenter sacked by the Taleban. She broadcast the first words after the fall of Kabul.*

I looked out of the window and there was smoke all over the place. I thought "Oh God, not again"
– *Sir Paul McCartney, who saw the World Trade Center attack as he was flying into New York, on then seeing the Airbus crash when he was a passenger on Concorde.*

Harry Potter is the don and playing Harry Potter will get him all the ladies
– *Charlotte Church, the teenage Welsh singer, on the film's star, Daniel Radcliffe.*

The footballers are going on strike? When can they start?
– *Letter to* The Times.

QPR, the team I support, withdrew their labour a season ago
– *Letter to* The Times.

Women want light entertainment and football is not light entertainment
– *Cilla Black.*

I used to have a "respectable" job as a nurse; now I take my clothes of for a living
– *Nichola Provart who earns more in one night as a lap dancer than in a month with the NHS.*

I am like my garden: my brain has been mulched and manured, things have grown and I am more complicated
– *Jonathan Miller.*

It is equally unpleasant to be surrounded by such overwhelming American patriotism day after day in support of a war against a regime many had never heard of until two months ago
– *Letter to* The Guardian *from a Briton in New York, on Chelsea Clinton's complaint about anti-American sentiment at Oxford.*

Regret
– *Chairman of Marconi on his company's world record-breaking annual loss of £5.1 billion.*

Don't tell Tony I used that word
– *John Reid, Northern Ireland Secretary, after addressing a Belfast audience as "comrades".*

Religion is like the weather. It can be good; it can also be very bad
– *Jonathan Sacks, The Chief Rabbi.*

The programme is producing valuable scientific information
– *Japan's Institute of Cetacean Research, on an expedition to kill 440 minke whales.*

Despicable
– *Government of New Zealand on the whaling expedition.*

I like to make intelligent films, but they are the most difficult because people want explosions. Bombs and bottoms are just not my thing
– *Mick Jagger.*

If the allegations of alcoholism, violence and paedophilia continue, we will consider further action
– *Teachers' union on comments left on a school reunion website.*

Class is just too dull for words
– *The Duchess of Devonshire.*

Week ending November 24, 2001

There was blood everywhere, but it wasn't mine
– *Cambridge PhD student Jessica Hudson on the bout that made her the first woman to box for a British university.*

I'm not even interested in aeroplanes
– *Lesley Coppin, incarcerated in Greece on spying charges after accompanying her husband on a plane-spotting holiday.*

There are far more important things which cause real harm to the community in the way that Ecstasy does not
– *Metropolitan Police Commander Brian Paddick tells a Commons committee why weekend drug-users are low on his priority list.*

Tony Blair is the best friend I've had in politics ▼
– *Gordon Brown.*

It is often a gateway into other spiritualities, including Eastern mysticism
– *Rev Richard Farr, vicar of Henham, Essex, on why he has banned yoga from his church hall.*

We want to stay British for ever
– *Gibraltarians' reaction to Anglo-Spanish talks to resolve the 300-year-old dispute over the Rock.*

People here are not very interested in what happens in continental Europe
– *Diplomat magazine on why two-thirds of foreign ambassadors and attachés find it hard to make British friends in London.*

It's really the result of talking to trees once too often
– *The Prince of Wales, wearing a large patch on his left eye after getting sawdust in it.*

You plan your days around the noise. We get effluent from the planes' toilets falling on us. People have had breakdowns
– *Pamela Armstrong, who lives near Heathrow, on why she opposed Terminal Five.*

Four-and-twenty naughty boys
– *Discovery of a 250-year-old book of nursery rhymes reveals that there was something more macabre than blackbirds in that pie.*

There are two Mujahidin and six Russians and two of the Russians are killed; how many are left?
– *Afghan maths textbook question.*

You can argue about that until the cows come home
– *Environment Minister Elliot Morley, during a radio debate with angry farmers*

about the slaughter of animals during the foot-and-mouth outbreak.

Pig-ignorant peasants
– *Nigel de Gruchy, teachers' union leader, on proposed classroom assistants.*

Is there a law which dictates that those who hold tickets for the centre seats in the row at the theatre always arrive last?
– *Letter to* The Times.

I really hope I'm going to become a porn baroness
– *Rowan Pelling, editor of* The Erotic Review.

This pile of steaming ordure dumped on the London travelling public is sheer official sabotage
– *Simon Jenkins on Government plans for the London Underground.*

Week ending December 1, 2001

She cannot defend her own rights against her husband. How can she defend the rights of my country?
– *Suhaila Siddiq, Afghanistan's only woman general, on Hillary Clinton's championing of Afghan womenhood.*

I'm not some mad career monster
– *TV presenter Fiona Bruce on returning to work 16 days after having a baby.*

They were all killed, and very few were arrested
– *Northern Alliance spokesman on the prisoners' revolt at the Qalai Janghi fort.*

This country is being targeted by the cloning industry. They are going to flock here
– *Pro-Life Alliance calls for tighter legislation after the first human embryo is cloned.*

I was so happy they put me on a psychiatric ward
– *Sandra Gregory, on being transferred from a Thai prison to Holloway.*

Humankind is fundamentally idle and that is one of our real problems
– *The Princess Royal on fast food.*

Nice to see the spirit of Sherlock Holmes lives on
– *Letter to* The Times, *on a police statement that the discovery of a woman's body in a suitcase is being treated as "suspicious".*

Marriage is no longer seen as having any advantage over cohabitation in everyday life
– *British Social Attitudes survey report.*

I don't think things are too bad here; only a few of my friends have been mugged and had their mobiles stolen
– *Resident of the London estate where Damilola Taylor, 10, was stabbed to death a year ago.*

Sharon Stone syndrome
– *Doctors identify a potentially dangerous threat to fortysomethings who suddenly take up vigorous exercise.*

It's a bit like being poor, but having a hell of a lot of money

– *The actor Griff Rhys Jones on being a millionaire.*

What sort of outfit is that? He looks like a bloody German
– *Tory MP Nicholas Soames on Foreign Office Minister Denis MacShane's grey flannels and dark blue blazer.*

I also experienced a unique sense of licence when anonymously taking possession of a fresh city from which I would be departing the same night
– *Moors murder Ian Brady, who describes planning his crimes as "acutely stimulating".*

An Arctic seal is to be transported free of charge in a wooden crate in an unheated carriage of a Virgin train. Is this a one-off or is the entire fleet to be upgraded to this standard?
– *Letter to* The Times.

I used to be but I gave it up because it made my eyes water
– *Actor Michael Gambon to an inquirer who assumed (mistakenly) that he was homosexual.*

Train crew displacement
– *Thameslink's euphemism for its failure to provide a driver.*

Week ending December 8, 2001

Is it not fortunate that Fanny Cradock did not achieve the same iconic status as Delia?
– *Letter to* The Times.

We wanted to portray them as innocents
— *Dylan Jones, editor of GQ, which featured a nude portrait of Christine and Neil Hamilton posing as Adam and Eve.*

I felt at the time I was simply part of a quite friendly group activity
— *Paul Galea, a consultant charged with improper behaviour towards nurses at Wigan infirmary.*

Kids do that all the time
— *Lifeguard Julie Blayney, when informed by a teacher that Anthony Armstrong, seven, had been underwater for a few minutes and wasn't moving.*

It was destroyed in a police raid
— *Excuse used to explain the failure to hand in homework, from a Europe-wide survey of teachers.*

We were not in an exclusive relationship. She has chosen single parenthood
— *Billionaire Steven Bing on the news that his girlfriend Elizabeth Hurley had become pregnant.*

He did not go to make war against his own country
— *Frank Lindh, father of John Walker, an American captured with Taleban fighters.*

George was a giant
— *Bob Dylan on the late George Harrison.*

She isn't mad about her teeth showing. And no profiles. What Jennifer really likes is a picture of herself smirking slightly. She likes to smirk
— *Conditions that publications must accept if they wish to photograph actress Jennifer Aniston.*

For a simple urban boy like me the idea of listening to three Somerset folk-singers sounds like hell
— *Kim Howells, parliamentary under-secretary for the Department of Culture, Media and Sport.*

Our music is for people fed up with listening to people like Kim Howells talking a lot of dung in the Commons
— *Tommy Banner, The Wurzels' accordionist.*

Everybody feels bad when they lose their son. But we are proud of him. You should be proud of him
— *Adel Habashi to his cousin, the father of one of the suicide bombers who blew up a bus in Haifa, killing 15 people and injuring 36.*

I could no more live in a village than make my bed in a wardrobe
— *Germaine Greer.*

I was able to start a high-fashion shop because two gentlemen were outbidding each other for my hot little body
— *Newly revealed comment by Gabrielle Chanel, on the origin of the couture house of Chanel.*

Body-piercing? Jesus had his done
2000 years ago
*– Message on a poster put out by the
Diocese of Birmingham, aimed at young
people.*

They stiffen but they do not curtsey
*– Reported comment by the Queen on
Cherie Blair's knees.*

Week ending December 15, 2001

I loved it when the wizards had their
fight. I like a good fight
*– Kym Marsh of Hear'Say after the
premiere of the film* The Lord of the
Rings.

It is a Harry Potter figure and it's not
on
*– Union leader on Consignia's decision to
cut 30,000 jobs.*

I can't explain it except to say that
the lights are definitely on and off
*– Martin Creed, awarded the Turner
Prize for an empty room in which the
lights go on and off every five seconds.*

If there is a power cut, is it still art?
– Letter to The Times.

At a time when political correctness
is valued over honesty, I would
just like to say "Right on, mother-
******"
– Madonna, presenting the Turner Prize.

There have been a couple of books
written about me by critics, but I
don't read them because I don't want
to know what my work is about
– Alan Bennett.

A modest grasp of the English tongue
*– The Home Secretary on an
accomplishment which would help
immigrants feel more British.*

The onset of old age wasn't
immediately obvious to me. A
doctor asked me if I was short of
breath when I took exercise, to
which I had to reply that I didn't
know, as I had never taken exercise
– Sir John Mortimer.

I'd rather go to the cinema in the
afternoon with the OAPs
*– Dame Diana Rigg on why she does
not attend film premieres.*

I see us as professional objects of
curiosity
*– Neil Hamilton of himself and his wife
Christine.*

We have a BBC safety hazards form
that we fill in before any production,
but being kissed by Christine
Hamilton didn't come into that
unfortunately
*– Louis Theroux, who made a
documentary on the Hamiltons.*

It happened a week after the terrorist
attacks on New York and everyone
looked so glum that I wanted to
cheer them up
– Football referee Brian Savill, facing

disciplinary charges for scoring a goal to help a losing non-league side.

Being the mother of a sex symbol is not sexy
– *Tessa Dahl, 43, mother of the model Sophie Dahl.*

I'd like to design people's gardens
– *Ken Livingstone on his retirement plans.*

Mud wrestling
– *Robin Cook on the public perception of party politics.*

They leave politics – with one or two rare exceptions – to the second rate, the incorrigibly bossy and the slightly weird
– *Author Robert Harris on young people's preference for careers in the media.*

Week ending December 22, 2001

It took a team of translators a week to figure out that "bangers and mash" were not some veiled British threat.
– *Former President Bill Clinton recalling the BBC's first experimental broadcast to the US in 1923.*

Until we catch bin Laden, which we will, we won't know precisely where he was
– *US Defense Secretary, Donald Rumsfeld.*

It's nothing to do with conservation or sustainable use.
– *Kew Garden explains that it is using plastic Christmas trees this year because they light up better.*

If I were going to go out with anyone for their money, I would be with someone a lot richer
– *Heather Mills on her fiancé, Sir Paul McCartney, who is worth £700 million.*

That shitty little country Israel
– *French Ambassador's reported remark at a London dinner party.*

The Ambassador does not remember if he used those words
– *French Embassy, London.*

The organisers were hoping for Jeffrey Archer, but unfortunately Jeffrey had put the wrong date in his diary; well, to be more exact, he had put the date in the wrong diary.
– *Rory Bremner at an award-presenting ceremony.*

Every soldier loathes bureaucracy. I was not going to muck around and bend over for some little official on the ground floor
– *Sir David Ramsbotham, former Chief Inspector of Prisons.*

Carruthers loves mothers. For his afternoon nap, he curls up in Gran's lap
– *From Ann Widdecombe's Christmas ode to her cat.*

Does having an Action Man doll dressed in a pink tutu on top of the Christmas tree this year concur with equal opportunities?
– *Letter to* The Times.

You cannot have a trade summit these days without tear gas. It would be like having a cheeseburger without cheese
– *White House official.*

The problem with beauty is that it is like being born rich and getting poorer
– *Four-times-wed Joan Collins at her engagement to Percy Gibson.*

2002

Week ending January 5, 2002

Where is Windsor and can I walk there?
— *Mariah Carey, singer, at Claridge's Hotel.*

Europhoria
— *Coinage to describe the general enthusiasm for the coinage.*

Democracies don't prepare well for things that have never happened before
— *Richard Clarke, former White House counterterrorism chief.*

I notice the trend to carry small bottles of water around. If this was Florence in August one could understand it. But London in December? Is this a fashion statement I need to catch up with?
— *Letter to* The Times.

Vegetarians are like animal rights protesters: they cannot just get on with their chosen, dreary approach to life. They have to scream at the rest of us as if this is going to bring us to our senses
— *Janet Street-Porter.*

He was not quite what I had in mind
— *Megan Holman, 87, mother of Christine Hamilton, on first meeting her son-in-law Neil Hamilton.*

If a man becomes a woman or a woman becomes a man, if they are priests they remain priests willy-nilly
— *The Bishop of Winchester, the Rt Rev Michael Scott-Joynt, on transsexual clergy.*

If everybody flew naked not only would you never have to worry about the passenger next to you having explosive shoes, but no religious fundamentalist would ever fly nude or in the presence of nude women
— *Thomas Friedman,* New York Times *columnist.*

I am very old-fashioned. I think wars are for men. Women on ships has been a disaster
— *Max Hastings, editor of London's* Evening Standard.

The whole bizarre panoply of OBEs, MBEs, CBEs, DCVOs, MVOs, GCBs, CHs, MNOGs and Yeomen Bed Goers should be put on the bonfire along with the vanity of those who care for such distinctions
— *Philip Collins, director of the Social Market Foundation.*

This information is handwritten in the interest of speeding up our customer service
— *Letter sent by insurance company Scottish Widows.*

The doctors say that I have chicken-pox quite mildly for a grown-up but it is not much consolation when one is covered in spots
— *Letter written by the Queen to the then Prime Minister Edward Heath in 1971, released under the 30-year rule.*

This is a moment for a little New Year's resolution, perhaps?
— *Liberal Democrat leader Charles Kennedy urging the Prime Minister to be bold about the euro.*

We love the place. Why would we want to stay away?
— *John Carey, one of 3,000 travellers, members of seven families, criticised for "invading" Bournemouth for a Christmas gathering.*

Week ending January 12, 2002

I don't want ever to look at myself and see the Joker from *Batman* staring back at me
— Sex in the City *actress Kim Cattrall rules out plastic surgery.*

I'm not a facelift person. You end up looking body-snatched
— *Robert Redford.*

La cuisine facile d'aujourd'hui
— *Delia Smith is translated into French.*

The French are proud and highly xenophobic when it comes to cooking. They don't take any advice well, but from a British woman?

French people are interested in the kind of picturesque awfulness of British food
— *François Simon, restaurant critic for* Le Figaro.

If Welsh is the language of heaven, why does it have irregular verbs?
— *Letter to* The Times.

A 24-carat crack-up
— *Downing Street adviser Alastair Campbell on his nervous breakdown.*

I haven't been tiddly since my 60th birthday. I don't think being drunk is very pretty in older people
— *Broadcaster Joan Bakewell, 68.*

I've decided I'm not old-fashioned enough to be Queen
— *The Queen.*

I think I could say that like myself, Her Majesty prefers animals to human beings. For one thing, they don't talk so much
— *Sir John Miller, former Crown Equerry in charge of the Royal Mews.*

F★★★★★★ piss off, Postlethwaite
— *Prince William charms a freelance photographer who attempted to photograph him returning from a morning's foxhunting.*

My son Edward is studying alien psychology, as it relates to humanity, at the University of California. I think you could call it a niche market
— *Actor David Hemmings.*

Believing in God's one thing, but I get a wee bit bored of angels. It's a wee bit in the aromatherapy field for me
– *Billy Connolly.*

He's very good-looking and very rich. He's a fantastic footballer with an attractive wife and a lovely child. He has what everyone wants – so therefore everyone hates him
– *Robbie Williams on David Beckham.*

A testimonial strike
– *South West Trains boss on a strike in support of a single rail union activist, which disrupted the lives of 200,000 commuters a day.*

The trick is to offer the least offence to the greatest number of people
– *Church House insider on bishops manoeuvring to succeed the Archbishop of Canterbury.*

I have made very little attempt to cure any of my bad habits over the years but the habit of running second in a Tory leadership campaign is one you should break eventually
– *Kenneth Clarke.*

Week ending January 19, 2002

Nothing would excite a young person more than the ability to buy, buy, buy and being famous. Contributing to society is not what it is about any more. Image is everything
– *Susie Orbach.*

There is no point hiding the truth. These are the facts. Let people make their own judgment
– *Prince Charles on Prince Harry's cannabis smoking.*

The job of protection officers is to protect the Princes, not mother them
– *St James's Palace on why Prince Harry's escort did not prevent his drug-taking and drinking.*

We are in worse shape than ever before, in my lifetime or yours. We are seen by many voters as racist, sexist, homophobic and anti-youth
– *John Bercow MP on the Tory party.*

It's not going to be a country club but it is going to be humane
– *US Defense Secretary Donald Rumsfeld on the conditions in which captured Taleban fighters are being held.*

I have opinions of my own – strong opinions – but I don't always agree with them
– *President George W. Bush.*

As couples try to be more entertaining they produce moves that are gynaecological, which is about as politely as it can be put
– *National Ice Skating Association asks competitors to tone down their acts.*

Fame is like a big piece of meringue – it's beautiful and you keep eating it, but it doesn't really fill you up
– *Pierce Brosnan.*

Madonna hates being called Madge. We're under strict instructions not to call her that
– *Jason Flemyng, actor*

They are ridiculously heavy even when they are empty. Most people fill them with copies of *Private Eye*
– *Lord Williams of Mostyn, Leader of the House of Lords, on ministerial red boxes.*

Queen Victoria had a habit of giving her knickers as presents to her ladies-in-waiting. They have definitely been worn and they're huge
– *Ann Wise, a curator at Worthing Museum exhibiting the royal undies.*

The actors were so bad I even had to dub their breathing
– *David Bailey, photographer, recalling his first feature film.*

If wealth does not bring happiness it allows one to be miserable in comfort
– *Letter to* The Times.

Liquidly
– *Pat Cox, when asked how he would celebrate his election as the European Parliament's new president.*

It is the equivalent of saying that if Napoleon had conquered Britain and then sold bits of Stonehenge to an Italian friend, then the French would have a claim to Stonehenge

– *Richard Allan MP, arguing for the Elgin Marbles to go back to Athens.*

Week ending January 26, 2002

There is nobody more boring than the undefeated. Any great, long career has at last one flame-out in it
– *Tina Brown on the demise of her magazine* Talk.

There's nothing more boring than a really beautiful person who has nothing to say
– *Gwyneth Paltrow.*

A duck-faced liability
– Times *critic Sean Macaulay on Penelope Cruz's performance opposite Tom Cruise in* Vanilla Sky.

Silly mistakes . . . must do better
– *John Kerr, chief of the Edexcel exam board, apologises for a series of errors.*

When they are being moved from place to place, will they be restrained in a way so that they are less likely to be able to kill an American soldier? You bet. Is it humane to do that? No. Would it be stupid to do anything else? Yes
– *Secretary of Defense Donald H. Rumsfeld, on al-Qaeda prisoners being held in Cuba.*

Small Round Structured Virus
– *Technical name for the bug causing a nationwide outbreak of gastric flu.*

I am not going to complain if people say it is going to be a bit bleak
– *Buckingham Palace source on fears that the Queen's Golden Jubilee celebrations will flop.*

None of my Governments seem to know what to do about them
– *Reported remark by the Queen in a discussion about recessions.*

They would be a lot more honest if they simply poured pots of paint over Volvos and BMWs. That's closer to what they are all about: a them–and–us situation
– *Anne Robinson says anti-hunt campaigners are more concerned with envy than animal welfare.*

Hello, Sinn Fein, Westminster
– *Gerry Adams, answering the phone at the House of Commons.*

Luxury disgusts me
– *Giorgio Armani.*

I don't even understand offside so I'm not likely to understand a Manchester United contract
– *Victoria Beckham on her husband David's career move.*

The first duty of the comedian is to offend. There are some bits of the Koran which can be very funny
– *Lord Desai.*

He bit my foot, he bit my foot – I can't believe he just bit my foot

– *Britain's world heavyweight champion boxer Lennox Lewis after a press-conference brawl with boxer Mike Tyson.*

How dare anyone suggest that a 94-year-old lady should be saying anything but the truth
– *The grandson of Rose Addis who is at the centre of the latest NHS row on Tony Blair's rejection of the family's complaint of poor treatment.*

I don't know what normal is
– *Lady Archer.*

When the cats are sick I clear that up, and I do know where the vacuum cleaner is
– *Jonathan Dimbleby on his contribution to the housework.*

Week ending Feburary 2, 2002

The chicest man on the planet
– *Designer Tom Ford on Hamid Karzai, interim leader of Afghanistan.*

We need to work with the Stans
– *International Development Secretary Clare Short on central Asian countries.*

I want to be a somebody, not die nobody in a dump like this
– *Asif Iqbal, a Briton being held at Camp X-Ray, Guantanamo, on his West Midlands home town, Tipton.*

When you get done, you get done
– *Stephen King announces his retirement from writing.*

Sheffield Labour Party has no plans whatsoever to commemorate the Jubilee
– *Vivien Nicholson, agent of Richard Caborn, the minister responsible for the celebrations.*

The whole idea of Golden Jubilee celebrations is out of date. It is part of the myth of Merrie England
– *Lord Hattersley.*

The Netherlands is painting itself orange for Saturday
– *De Telegraaf newspaper on the Dutch enthusiasm for the nuptials of Máxima Zorreguieta and Prince Willem-Alexander.*

No one takes the suburbs seriously, and people who write about them always patronise them, and look down on them morally
– *Michael Frayn.*

I'm not the Ancient Mariner
– *Sir Paul McCartney.*

In Los Angeles everyone has perfect teeth. It's crocodile land
– *Gwyneth Paltrow.*

I've become more masculine. It's such a relief
– *Joanna Trollope.*

Snobbishness is merely a deprecatory synonym of discrimination
– *Jonathan Meades on being asked whether he is a snob.*

I'm crazy but I'm not crazy like that. I'm not Mother Teresa and I'm not Charles Manson either
– *Mike Tyson, boxer.*

Have you started taking cannabis yet?
– *Prince Charles to multiple-sclerosis sufferer in Wales.*

Boasting, self-revelation and self-promotion are in. Modesty, discretion and humility are out. Britons have never been so self-obsessed or so self-promoting
– *Jonathan Aitken.*

Money – the one thing that keeps us in touch with our children
– *Gyles Brandreth.*

There was quite a loud shout when it went in
– *Chris Higgins, 55, on his second hole-in-one in a single round of golf.*

She is a hero
– *Wasfiya Idris, on her daughter Wafa'a Ali Idris, the first female suicide bomber.*

He deserves as much respect as anyone else. He is not dishonest
– *William Archer on his father, Lord Archer, convicted for perjury.*

Modulation
– *The buzzword for shifting farm subsidy from food development to rural development and conservation.*

Who Said What . . .